Control of substances hazardous to health (Fifth edition)

The Control of Substances Hazardous
to Health Regulations 2002 (as amended)

Approved Code of Practice and guidance

HSE Books

D0480762

The Approved Code of Practice and guidance

This Code has been approved by the Health and Safety Commission, with the consent of the Secretary of State. It gives practical advice on how to comply with the law. If you follow the advice you will be doing enough to comply with the law in respect of those specific matters on which the Code gives advice. You may use alternative methods to those set out in the Code in order to comply with the law.

However, the Code has a special legal status. If you are prosecuted for breach of health and safety law, and it is proved that you did not follow the relevant provisions of the Code, you will need to show that you have complied with the law in some other way or a court will find you at fault.

The Regulations and Approved Code of Practice (ACOP) are accompanied by guidance which does not form part of the ACOP. Following the guidance is not compulsory and you are free to take other action. But if you do follow the guidance you will normally be doing enough to comply with the law. Health and safety inspectors seek to secure compliance with the law and may refer to this guidance as illustrating good practice.

Contents

Notice of Approval

By virtue of section 16(4) of the Health and Safety at Work etc Act 1974 ('the 1974 Act'), and with the consent of the Secretary of State for Work and Pensions pursuant to section 16(2) of the 1974 Act, the Health and Safety Commission has on 24 March 2005 approved the revised Code of Practice entitled Control of substances hazardous to health (Fifth edition, 2005, L5, ISBN 0 7176 2981 3).

The revised Code of Practice comes into force on 6 April 2005.

The Code of Practice gives practical guidance on the Control of Substances Hazardous to Health Regulations 2002 (as amended by the Control of Substances Hazardous to Health (Amendment) Regulations 2003 and the Control of Substances Hazardous to Health (Amendment) Regulations 2004).

By virtue of section 16(5) of the 1974 Act and with the consent of the Secretary of State under that paragraph, the Health and Safety Commission has withdrawn the Code of Practice entitled Control of substances hazardous to health (Fourth edition, 2002, L5, ISBN 0 7176 2534 6) approved by the Commission on 11 November 2002, which ceased to have effect on 6 April 2005, being the date the relevant amendments made by the Control of Substances Hazardous to Health (Amendment) Regulations 2004 came into force.

Signed

SUSAN MAWER
Secretary to the Health and Safety Commission

24 March 2005

Introduction

1   This publication contains the Approved Code of Practice (ACOP) for the Control of Substances Hazardous to Health Regulations 2002[1] (as amended by the Control of Substances Hazardous to Health (Amendment) Regulations 2003[2] and the Control of Substances Hazardous to Health (Amendment) Regulations 2004).[3] It includes appendices which provide supporting guidance on the control of carcinogenic and mutagenic substances; additional provisions relating to work with biological agents; and on the control of substances that cause occupational asthma. The ACOP applies to all substances to which the Control of Substances Hazardous to Health Regulations 2002 (COSHH) apply.

2   The content of the ACOP has been revised to comply with the Health and Safety Commission's statement on the role and status of ACOPs, which it published in February 1996. Accordingly, the ACOP text now concentrates on giving practical guidance and methods of complying with goal-setting regulations, on what is considered reasonably practicable and on advised, but not mandatory, methods of meeting legal obligations.

3   Additional Codes of Practice have been approved in respect of certain substances, processes and activities. These give supplementary advice to this ACOP and should be referred to where relevant.

4   For convenience, in this publication, the ACOP text is set out in **bold** and the accompanying guidance in normal type, while the text of COSHH is in *italics*. Coloured borders also indicate each section clearly.

Summary of changes to the Regulations

Summary of main changes in COSHH 2002

5   These Regulations (SI 2002/2677) revoked the earlier COSHH 1999. The main changes introduced by the 2002 Regulations result from the requirement to implement EC Directive (98/24/EC) *Protection of the health and safety of workers from the risks related to chemical agents at work*.[4] Other changes result from transposing some of the requirements in Schedule 3 to COSHH 1999 (Special provisions relating to biological agents) to the main body of the Regulations.

6   The main changes made by the 2002 Regulations were:

(a)   new definitions: 'approved classification' (ie of a biological agent); 'the CHIP Regulations';[5] 'control measure'; 'hazard'; 'medical examination'; 'personal protective equipment'; 'public road'; 'relevant doctor'; 'risk'; 'risk assessment'; 'safety data sheet'; and 'workplace' in regulation 2;

(b)   the definitions of 'biological agent', 'inhalable dust', 'respirable dust' and 'substance hazardous to health' have been amended in regulation 2;

(c)   the definitions of 'appointed doctor', 'employment medical adviser' and 'health surveillance' have been transposed from regulation 11, and that of 'health surveillance' extended in regulation 2;

(d)   the definitions of 'cell culture' and 'Group' have been transposed from Schedule 3 to regulation 2;

(e)   the provision relating to biological agents in Schedule 3 paragraph 3(2) has been transposed to regulation 2(3);

(f)   a reference to a new regulation 13 dealing with accidents has been inserted into regulation 3(1)(b);

(g) a reference to the Coal Mines (Respirable Dust) Regulations 1975[6] has been inserted into regulation 5(1)(a), and a reference to 'or other person who is an appropriate practitioner for the purposes of section 58 of the Medicines Act 1968'[7] has been inserted into regulation 5(2);

(h) regulation 6 on the assessment has been substantially extended to require that:

   (i)   the steps identified by the assessment to meet the requirements of the Regulations are implemented (regulation 6(1)(b));

   (ii)   the assessment is to consider a specific list of items (regulation 6(2)). (Item k) is transposed from Schedule 3 paragraph 4);

   (iii) the assessment is to be reviewed if the results of any monitoring show it to be necessary (regulation 6(3)(c));

   (iv)   employers, who employ five or more employees, record the significant findings of the assessment as soon as is practicable after the risk assessment is made and take steps to meet the requirements of regulation 7 (regulation 6(4));

(i) regulation 7 has been substantially extended:

   (i)   a specific requirement to prevent exposure to a substance hazardous to health by substituting a substance or process which eliminates or reduces the risk to the health of employees has been inserted into regulation 7(2);

   (ii)   a list of control measures to be applied in order of priority has been inserted in regulation 7(3);

   (iii) the requirements relating to biological agents in Schedule 3 paragraph 6 have been transposed to regulation 7(6);

(j) a new requirement to keep all control measures (and not just personal protective equipment), where relevant, in a clean condition has been added to regulation 9(1);

(k) the requirements relating to biological agents in Schedule 3 paragraph 9(1), (2) and (3) have been transposed to regulation 9(5), (6) and (7) and extended to all substances hazardous to health;

(l) a new provision setting out that an employer can use methods other than monitoring exposure to demonstrate compliance with regulation 7(1) is in regulation 10(2);

(m) a new requirement setting out when monitoring of employees' exposure should take place has been added in regulation 10(3);

(n) a new requirement clarifying how long employers should keep exposure records has been added to the end of regulation 10(5);

(o) a new requirement for employers to keep individual records of monitoring in certain circumstances is in regulation 10(6);

(p) new requirements for the employer to make monitoring records available in certain circumstances have been added in regulation 10(7);

(q) the words 'unless that exposure is not significant' have been replaced by 'and there is a reasonable likelihood that an identifiable disease or adverse health effect will result from that exposure' in regulation 11(2)(a);

(r) a further condition on when health surveillance is appropriate has been inserted at the end of regulation 11(2);

(s) a new requirement for the employer to make health records available to HSE in regulation 11(4)(b);

(t) new requirements on the employer when health surveillance reveals an employee to have an identifiable disease or adverse health effect resulting from exposure to a substance hazardous to health are in regulation 11(9);

(u) regulation 12 on information, instruction and training has been extended:

   (i) it covers the specific list of items in regulation 12(2)(a)-(c);

   (ii) the requirements relating to Group 4 biological agents in regulation 12(2)(f) have been transposed from Schedule 3 paragraph 10(1)(b);

   (iii) a new requirement on when the information, instruction and training is adapted and how it should be provided is in regulation 12(3);

   (iv) a requirement for the contents of containers and pipes used for substances hazardous to health to be identified is in regulation 12(5);

(v) new requirements to deal with accidents, incidents and emergencies are in regulation 13. The requirement in regulation 13(2)(b) has been transposed from Schedule 3 paragraph 10(1) (which applied solely to biological agents) and extended to all substances hazardous to health; and the requirements in regulation 13(3)(c) and (5) have been transposed from Schedule 3 paragraphs 10(3) and 10(2) respectively.

Changes made by the COSHH (Amendment) Regulations 2003

(w) These Regulations (SI 2003/978) came into force on 29 April 2003. They added a definition of 'mutagen' (regulation 2(1)) and extended to mutagens certain provisions of COSHH (in regulations 7(5) and 13(4)) that formerly related only to carcinogens or biological agents. In addition, 17 'dioxins' were included in Schedule 1 of COSHH to make clear that these substances are carcinogenic within the meaning of the Regulations.

Changes made by the COSHH (Amendment) Regulations 2004

(x) These Regulations (SI 2004/3386) came into force on 17 January 2005 (in respect of restrictions relating to cement and a revision of the disapplication of COSHH to merchant ships) and on 6 April 2005 (in respect of a new framework for adequate control of exposure and of a clarificatory revision of the duty to maintain exposure control measures). They:

   (i) prohibit the supply and use of cement and cement preparations containing more than 0.0002% of soluble chromium (VI) measured with respect to the dry weight of the cement and, where a reducing agent has been used, require that packages of cement and cement preparations be marked with information on packing date, storage period and recommended storage conditions;

(ii) disapply COSHH to all merchant ships (including non-sea-going merchant ships) in specified circumstances;

(iii) introduce a new framework for adequate control of exposure by specifying principles of good practice (Schedule 2A) and by replacing occupational exposure standards (OESs) and maximum exposure limits (MELs) with workplace exposure limits (WELs); and

(iv) clarify the wording of the duty to maintain exposure control measures so as to make clear that the scope of the duty extends to methods of work and supervision in addition to plant and equipment.

Summary of changes to the ACOP

Changes to the ACOP

7   This new fifth edition of the COSHH ACOP has been produced in response to the COSHH (Amendment) Regulations 2004. There are a considerable number of changes to the ACOP, most of which relate to the new framework for adequate control of exposure to substances hazardous to health.

8   In summary, the changes are as follows:

(a)   in connection with the new framework:

(i) extensive alterations and additions to the paragraphs following regulation 7 (see paragraphs 89–157);

(ii) revision of two paragraphs following regulation 10 (see paragraphs 204-205);

(iii) addition of guidance on the application of the principles of good practice for control of exposure to substances hazardous to health following Schedule 2A (see paragraphs 295-357); and

(iv) additional text in paragraph 12 of Appendix 3 (Control of substances that cause occupational asthma).

(b)   other changes include:

(i) revision of a number of paragraphs following regulation 9 (see paragraphs 160–162, 164, 170 and addition of a new paragraph 188); and

(ii) replacement of 'carcinogen' by 'carcinogen or mutagen' in various paragraphs of Appendix 1 to reflect a change made by COSHH 2003;

Consulting employees and safety representatives

9   Proper consultation with those who do the work is crucial in helping to raise awareness of the importance of health and safety. It can make a significant contribution to creating and maintaining a safe and healthy working environment and an effective health and safety culture. In turn, this can benefit the business by making it more efficient by reducing the number of accidents and the incidents of work-related ill health.

10 Employers must consult safety representatives appointed by recognised trade unions under the Safety Representatives and Safety Committees Regulations 1977.[8] Employees who are not covered by such representatives must be consulted, either directly or indirectly, through elected representatives of employee safety under the Health and Safety (Consultation with Employees) Regulations 1996. More information on an employer's duties under these Regulations is contained in the free HSE leaflet *Consulting employees on health and safety: A guide to the law*.[8]

Regulation 1

Regulation 1

Citation and commencement

These Regulations may be cited as the Control of Substances Hazardous to Health Regulations 2002 and shall come into force on 21 November 2002.

Regulation 2

Regulation

Interpretation

(1) In these Regulations –

"the 1974 Act" means the Health and Safety at Work etc Act 1974;

"the Agreement" means the Agreement on the European Economic Area signed at Oporto on 2nd May 1992 as adjusted by the Protocol signed at Brussels on 17th March 1993[(a)] and adopted as respects Great Britain by the European Economic Area Act 1993[(b)];

"appointed doctor" means a registered medical practitioner appointed for the time being in writing by the Executive for the purpose of these Regulations;

"approved" means approved for the time being in writing;

"approved classification" of a biological agent means the classification of that agent approved by the Health and Safety Commission;

"approved supply list" has the meaning assigned to it in regulation 2(1) of the CHIP Regulations;

"biological agent" means a micro-organism, cell culture, or human endoparasite, whether or not genetically modified, which may cause infection, allergy, toxicity or otherwise create a hazard to human health;

"carcinogen" means –

(a) a substance or preparation which if classified in accordance with the classification provided for by regulation 4 of the CHIP Regulations would be in the category of danger, carcinogenic (category 1) or carcinogenic (category 2) whether or not the substance or preparation would be required to be classified under those Regulations; or

(a) The Agreement was amended by Decision 7/94 of the EEA Joint Committee of 21st March 1994 (OJ No L160, 28.6.94, p.l). There are other amendments to the Agreement not relevant to these Regulations.
(b) 1993 c.51.

(b)   a substance or preparation –

(i)   listed in Schedule 1, or

(ii)   arising from a process specified in Schedule 1 which is a substance hazardous to health;

"cell culture" means the in-vitro growth of cells derived from multicellular organisms;

"the CHIP Regulations" means the Chemicals (Hazard Information and Packaging for Supply) Regulations 2002[(a)];

"control measure" means a measure taken to reduce exposure to a substance hazardous to health (including the provision of systems of work and supervision, the cleaning of workplaces, premises, plant and equipment, the provision and use of engineering controls and personal protective equipment;

"employment medical adviser" means an employment medical adviser appointed under section 56 of the Health and Safety at Work etc Act 1974;

"the Executive" means the Health and Safety Executive;

"fumigation" means an operation in which a substance is released into the atmosphere so as to form a gas to control or kill pests or other undesirable organisms and "fumigate" and "fumigant" shall be construed accordingly;

"Group", in relation to a biological agent, means one of the four hazard Groups specified in paragraph 2 of Schedule 3 to which that agent is assigned;

"hazard", in relation to a substance, means the intrinsic property of that substance which has the potential to cause harm to the health of a person, and "hazardous" shall be construed accordingly;

"health surveillance" means assessment of the state of health of an employee, as related to exposure to substances hazardous to health, and includes biological monitoring;

"inhalable dust" means airborne material which is capable of entering the nose and mouth during breathing, as defined by BS EN 481 1993;

"medical examination" includes any laboratory tests and X-rays that a relevant doctor may require;

"member State" means a State which is a Contracting Party to the Agreement;

"micro-organism" means a microbiological entity, cellular or non-cellular, which is capable of replication or of transferring genetic material;

"mine" has the meaning assigned to it by section 180 of the Mines and Quarries Act 1954[(b)];

(a) SI 2002/1689.
(b) 1954 c.70; section 180 was modified by SI 1974/2013, SI 1993/1897 and SI 1999/2024.

"mutagen" means a substance or preparation which if classified in accordance with the classification provided for by regulation 4 of the Chemicals (Hazard Information and Packaging for Supply) Regulations 2002 would be in the category of danger, mutagenic (category 1) or mutagenic (category 2) whether or not the substance or preparation would be required to be classified under those Regulations;

"personal protective equipment" means all equipment (including clothing) which is intended to be worn or held by a person at work and which protects that person against one or more risks to his health, and any addition or accessory designed to meet that objective;

"preparation" means a mixture or solution of two or more substances;

"public road" means (in England and Wales) a highway maintainable at the public expense within the meaning of section 329 of the Highways Act 1980[(a)] and (in Scotland) a public road within the meaning assigned to that term by section 151 of the Roads (Scotland) Act 1984[(b)];

"registered dentist" has the meaning assigned to it in section 53(1) of the Dentists Act 1984[(c)];

"relevant doctor" means an appointed doctor or an employment medical adviser;

"respirable dust" means airborne material which is capable of penetrating to the gas exchange region of the lung, as defined by BS EN 481 1993;

"risk", in relation to the exposure of an employee to a substance hazardous to health, means the likelihood that the potential for harm to the health of a person will be attained under the conditions of use and exposure and also the extent of that harm;

"the risk assessment" means the assessment of risk required by regulation 6(1)(a);

"risk phrase" has the meaning assigned to it in regulation 2(1) of the CHIP Regulations;

"safety data sheet" means a safety data sheet within the meaning of regulation 5 of the CHIP Regulations;

"substance" means a natural or artificial substance whether in solid or liquid form or in the form of a gas or vapour (including micro-organisms);

"substance hazardous to health" means a substance (including a preparation) –

(a)   which is listed in Part I of the approved supply list as dangerous for supply within the meaning of the CHIP Regulations and for which an indication of danger specified for the substance is very toxic, toxic, harmful, corrosive or irritant;

(b)   for which the Health and Safety Commission has approved a workplace exposure limit;

(a) 1980 c.66.
(b) 1984 c.54.
(c) 1984 c.24.

(c)   which is a biological agent;

(d)   which is dust of any kind, except dust which is a substance within paragraph (a) or (b) above, when present at a concentration in air equal to or greater than –

   (i)   10 mg/m^3, as a time-weighted average over an 8-hour period, of inhalable dust, or

   (ii)   4 mg/m^3, as a time-weighted average over an 8-hour period, of respirable dust;

(e)   which, not being a substance falling within sub-paragraphs (a) to (d), because of its chemical or toxicological properties and the way it is used or is present at the workplace creates a risk to health;

"workplace" means any premises or part of premises used for or in connection with work, and includes –

(a)   any place within the premises to which an employee has access while at work; and

(b)   any room, lobby, corridor, staircase, road or other place –

   (i)   used as a means of access to or egress from that place of work, or

   (ii)   where facilities are provided for use in connection with that place of work,

   other than a public road;

"workplace exposure limit" for a substance hazardous to health means the exposure limit approved by the Health and Safety Commission for that substance in relation to the specified reference period when calculated by a method approved by the Health and Safety Commission, as contained in HSE publication "EH/40 Workplace Exposure Limits 2005" as updated from time to time.

(2)   In these Regulations, a reference to an employee being exposed to a substance hazardous to health is a reference to the exposure of that employee to a substance hazardous to health arising out of or in connection with work at the workplace.

(3)   Where a biological agent has an approved classification, any reference in these Regulations to a particular Group in relation to that agent shall be taken as a reference to the Group to which that agent has been assigned in that approved classification.

Substances hazardous to health

11   COSHH 2002 applies to a very wide range of substances and preparations – mixtures of two or more substances – with the potential to cause harm if they are inhaled, ingested or come into contact with or are absorbed through the skin. These include individual chemical substances or preparations such as paints, cleaning materials, metals, pesticides and insecticides. They can also be biological agents such as pathogens or cell cultures. Substances hazardous to health can occur in many forms, eg solids, liquids, vapours, gases, dusts, fibres, fumes, mist and smoke.

12   Chemicals covered are those which, if classified under the Chemicals (Hazard Information and Packaging for Supply) Regulations 2002 (CHIP),[5] would be classified as very toxic, toxic, harmful, corrosive, irritant, sensitising, carcinogenic, mutagenic or toxic to reproduction. The terms 'carcinogen' and 'mutagen' have a wider meaning in CHIP than in COSHH. In COSHH these terms cover only substances and preparations which if classified under CHIP would be classified as carcinogenic (category 1 or category 2) or as mutagenic (category 1 or category 2). In COSHH the term 'carcinogen' also applies to substances and processes listed in Schedule 1.

13   Many commonly supplied substances, classified in one or more of the ways described above, are listed in Part I of the *Approved Supply List: Information approved for the classification and labelling of substances and preparations dangerous for supply*.[9] However, that document should not be regarded as a complete listing of chemicals covered by COSHH as it deals only with substances subject to CHIP and even then omits many substances and all preparations.

14   Substances which have been assigned WELs by the Health and Safety Commission (HSC) are also subject to the Regulations.

15   Dust of any kind can also become a substance hazardous to health under COSHH when it is present at concentrations in the air equal to or greater than 10 mg/m^3 (as a time-weighted average over an 8-hour period) of inhalable dust or 4 mg/m^3 (as a time-weighted average over an 8-hour period) of respirable dust. Good occupational hygiene practice recommends that those levels should be the highest concentrations of dust to which employees should be exposed. However, there may be dusts with no formal occupational exposure limit (OEL) and which are not listed in CHIP, but for which limits lower than 10 mg/m^3 or 4 mg/m^3 would be appropriate, because of evidence of potential hazards to health. For these dusts, employers are advised to set their own in-house standards.

16   The definitions of 'inhalable dust' and 'respirable dust' include references to BS EN 481: 1993 which relates to the British Standard *Workplace atmospheres. Size fraction definitions for measurement of airborne particles*.[10] This is the English language version of the European Standard approved by the European Committee for Standardization (CEN).

17   The 'catch-all' part of the definition of 'substance hazardous to health' in sub-paragraph (e) brings within the scope of the Regulations all other potentially hazardous substances not covered by the specific descriptions in sub-paragraphs (a)-(d). Although these will include other hazardous substances which may present only a very small risk in the workplace, an employer's main concern should be with those substances which may pose a risk comparable with those created by the substances covered by sub-paragraphs (a)-(d).

18   Employers should regard a substance as hazardous to health if it is hazardous in the form in which it may occur in the work activity. A substance hazardous to health need not be just a single chemical compound, but also includes mixtures of compounds, micro-organisms, allergens etc.

Asphyxiants

19   The revised text introduced into sub-paragraph (e) of the definition of a 'substance hazardous to health' brings within the scope of COSHH those gases and vapours which, when present at high concentrations in air at the workplace, act as simple asphyxiants. These can reduce the oxygen content to such an extent that life cannot be supported. Many of these asphyxiant gases are odourless and

colourless and not readily detectable. Therefore, monitoring the oxygen content of the air is a means of ensuring that their presence does not pose a risk to the health of employees.

20 Some of the gases concerned are extremely flammable and can present a risk of fire or explosion. Consequently, they are classified as dangerous for supply under CHIP and assigned a physicochemical category of danger 'extremely flammable' and included in Part I of CHIP's *Approved Supply List*.[9] These flammable asphyxiant gases satisfy the definition of 'dangerous substance' as set out in the Dangerous Substances and Explosive Atmospheres Regulations 2002 (DSEAR).[11] Where these gases are used in the workplace, employers will need to assess the risks they may pose to the health and safety of employees under both COSHH and DSEAR. In practice, the requirements of the Confined Spaces Regulations 1997[12] may also apply to the use of asphyxiant gases and employers may have further duties under those Regulations.

Biological agents

21 The definition of a 'biological agent' includes:

(a) micro-organisms such as bacteria, viruses, fungi, and the agents that cause transmissible spongiform encephalopathies (TSEs);

(b) parasites, eg malarial parasites, amoebae and trypanosomes; and

(c) the microscopic infectious forms of larger parasites, eg the microscopic ova and infectious larval forms of helminths;

providing they have one or more of the harmful properties specified in the definition (cause any infection, allergy, toxicity or otherwise create a hazard to human health). Most are infectious but some agents can be harmful in other ways, for example, via the production of toxins or by inducing allergic responses.

22 Biological agents are classified into four hazard groups according to:

(a) their ability to cause infection;

(b) the severity of the disease that may result;

(c) the risk that infection will spread to the community; and

(d) the availability of vaccines and effective treatment.

23 The four groups of biological agents and their accompanying descriptions are set out in paragraph 2(2) of Schedule 3 to these Regulations. Biological agents in Groups 2-4 are listed in a classification list approved by HSC (referred to as the *Approved list of biological agents*).[13] The Approved List is an electronic only publication found on the HSE website on the 'Infections at work' pages. The List is not exhaustive and a biological agent that does not appear on it does not automatically fall into Group 1. Even where a non-infectious biological agent does fall into Group 1, substantial control measures may still be needed for it, depending on its other harmful properties.

Carcinogens and mutagens

24 COSHH includes in regulation 7(5) special provisions for preventing or adequately controlling exposure to carcinogens and mutagens. For guidance on

risks from exposure to carcinogens and mutagens, employers should read this ACOP, together with the additional information in Appendix 1. Scientific research continues to find further substances and processes which it suspects, with varying degrees of confidence, of causing cancer or of causing heritable genetic damage. It is important, therefore, for employers to have an active precautionary policy of prevention and control based on up-to-date knowledge of the substances which are suspected of being carcinogenic or mutagenic, but which are not yet subject to the special provisions for carcinogens and mutagens contained in regulation 7 and Appendix 1.

25   The need for caution applies particularly to substances which have not previously been considered to be hazardous in this way, or perhaps in any way, since they are more likely to have been used without particular care. With all diseases, prevention is better than cure. Where the effects of exposure can be irreversible, prevention may be the only option.

Other points to consider

26   When deciding whether the substances used or produced in the workplace are covered by COSHH, employers should also consider the following:

(a)   different forms of a substance may present different hazards, eg substances may not be hazardous in solid form but may be hazardous when ground into fine powder or dust that can be breathed into the lungs;

(b)   impurities in a substance can make it more hazardous, eg crystalline silica is often present in minerals which would otherwise present little or no hazard;

(c)   some substances have a fibrous form which may present a potentially serious hazard to health, if the fibres are of a certain size or shape;

(d)   some substances have a known health effect, but the mechanism causing it is unknown, eg certain dusts of textile raw materials cause byssinosis;

(e)   exposure to two or more substances at the same time or one after the other may have an added or synergistic effect;

(f)   epidemiological or other data, eg reports of illness due to new and emerging agents, which indicate that a biological agent that does not already appear in the *Approved list of biological agents* could nevertheless cause a hazard to health;

(g)   one-off, emergency situations arising out of the work activity, such as a dangerous chemical reaction or fire which could foreseeably produce a substance hazardous to health.

The workplace

27   The definition of 'workplace' is based on that used in the Workplace (Health, Safety and Welfare) Regulations 1992[14] but is wider in scope as it also applies to domestic premises, ie private dwellings. Certain words in the definition are themselves defined in section 53 of the Health and Safety at Work etc Act 1974.

28   In particular, 'premises' means any place (whether or not there is a structure at that place). It includes vehicles, vessels, any land-based or offshore installations, movable areas to which employees have access while at work and their means of access to and exit from, the workplace. So, common parts of shared buildings,

private roads and paths on industrial estates and business parks are included. Public roads which are used to get to or from the workplace are not covered by the definition. However, in some circumstances, a public road may itself become the workplace, and if substances hazardous to health are used or produced during the work activity concerned, COSHH may apply, eg road repairing or resurfacing, kerbstone cutting, line painting etc.

Where to find out more about hazardous substances

29   There are many sources of information that employers can use to find out more about the hazardous properties of substances. These include:

(a)   labels and safety data sheets complying with CHIP or from self-classifying substances or preparations by applying the criteria in CHIP;

(b)   other information provided by the manufacturer or supplier of the substance under section 6 of the Health and Safety at Work etc Act 1974 (amended by the Consumer Protection Act 1987);[15]

(c)   the *Approved list of biological agents*;[13]

(d)   guidance published by the Health and Safety Executive (HSE) and the HSC or other authoritative organisations;

(e)   *Risk assessment reports* published by the European Union on specific chemical substances in connection with work carried out in accordance with Council Regulation (EEC) 793/93[16] on the evaluation and control of the risks of 'existing' substances;

(f)   previous experience of using the substance, similar substances, or agent;

(g)   technical reference sources (textbooks, scientific and technical papers, trade journals etc);

(h)   professional institutions, trade associations, trade unions and specialist consultancy services; and

(i)   the Internet.

Exposure arising out of or in connection with the workplace

30   In regulation 2(2), the former words ' *... arising out of or in connection with work which is under the control of his employer*' have been amended to read ' *... arising out of or in connection with work at the workplace*'. This change has been made to correct a potential weakness in COSHH. Sub-contractors working on a site where their employees are exposed to substances hazardous to health might not place their employees under health surveillance because, as sub-contractors, the work on the site is not under their overall control. Overall control of the day-to-day work on the site is more likely to be the responsibility of the main or co-ordinating contractor, who under regulation 3(1)(a) of COSHH has no legal duty to place under health surveillance people who are not the contractor's own employees.

31   In the circumstances described, it is the sub-contractor's duty to place their own employees under health surveillance where the assessments made under regulation 6(1) show it to be appropriate for the protection of the health of their employees. However, on larger sites, it is sometimes the custom and practice for

2

the main contractor in overall charge to arrange for health surveillance to be provided for all people working on the site who are exposed to hazardous substances. The amendment to regulation 2(2) is not intended to discourage this practice.

Regulation 3

Duties under these Regulations

(1)   Where a duty is placed by these Regulations on an employer in respect of his employees, he shall, so far as is reasonably practicable, be under a like duty in respect of any other person, whether at work or not, who may be affected by the work carried out by the employer except that the duties of the employer –

(a)   under regulation 11 (health surveillance) shall not extend to persons who are not his employees; and

(b)   under regulations 10, 12(1) and (2) and 13 (which relate respectively to monitoring, information and training and dealing with accidents) shall not extend to persons who are not his employees, unless those persons are on the premises where the work is being carried out.

(2)   These Regulations shall apply to a self-employed person as they apply to an employer and an employee and as if that self-employed person were both an employer and an employee, except that regulations 10 and 11 shall not apply to a self-employed person.

(3)   These Regulations shall not apply to the master or crew of a ship or to the employer of such persons in respect of the normal shipboard activities of a ship's crew which –

(a)   are carried out solely by the crew under the direction of the master; and

(b)   are not liable to expose persons other than the master and crew to a risk to their health and safety,

and for the purposes of this paragraph "ship" includes every description of vessel used in navigation, other than a ship forming part of Her Majesty's Navy.

Duties of employers

32   Employers include contractors, sub-contractors and self-employed people. Self-employed people have the duties of employers and employees except for the regulations relating to monitoring and health surveillance (regulations 10 and 11).

33   Table 1 summarises the scope of the employer's duties in respect of employees and other people likely to be affected by the work, eg visitors to a site, and where biological agents are concerned, patients in a hospital.

So far as is reasonably practicable

34   The term 'so far as is reasonably practicable' is used several times in this document, and needs to be clearly understood in the context of these Regulations. It has been interpreted by the courts as allowing economic considerations to be taken into account as one factor with, for example, time or trouble, to be set against the risk. It is reasonably practicable to take measures up to the point where the taking of further measures becomes grossly disproportionate to any residual risk. The greater the risk, the more likely it is that it is reasonable to go to

Table 1 The employer's duties

Duty of employer relating to:	Duty for the protection of:		
	Employees	Other people on the premises	Other people likely to be affected by work
Assessment (regulation 6)	Yes	SFAIRP	SFAIRP
Prevention or control of exposure (regulation 7)	Yes	SFAIRP	SFAIRP
Use of control measures and maintenance, examination and test of control measures (regulations 8 and 9)	Yes	SFAIRP	SFAIRP
Monitoring exposure at workplace (regulation 10)	Yes, where requisite	SFAIRP	No
Health surveillance (regulation 11)	Yes, where appropriate	No	No
Information, training etc (regulation 12)	Yes	SFAIRP	No
Arrangements to deal with accidents, incidents and emergencies (regulation 13)	Yes	SFAIRP	No
SFAIRP = So far as is reasonably practicable			

substantial expense, trouble and invention to reduce it. However, if the risk is small, it would not be considered reasonable to go to great expense. Ultimately, the judgement is an objective one based on the health risks and not on the size or financial position of the employer.

Working at another employer's premises

35   Contractors, sub-contractors and self-employed people all have the duties of employers under the Regulations. Where the employees of one employer work at another employer's premises, both employers have duties under the Regulations and also under the Management of Health and Safety at Work Regulations 1999 ('the Management regulations').[17] Each employer has duties to their own employees and, so far as is reasonably practicable, to the employees of the other employer.

The visiting employer

36   When working at another employer's premises, the two employers should co-operate and collaborate to ensure that all the duties imposed by COSHH are fulfilled. They may need to decide which of them will carry out a particular duty. For example, it is usually appropriate for the employer who creates the risk to carry out any necessary monitoring of exposure.

The employer occupying the premises

37   However, the employer occupying the premises should also provide the visiting employer with sufficient information about any substances hazardous to health that may be used or produced at the premises. The information provided by the occupier should be sufficiently detailed to allow the visiting employer to provide his own employees with information and any appropriate instruction on complying with the occupying employer's control measures.

38   The occupier of the premises will also need to know about any substances hazardous to health that are likely to be used or produced by the work the visiting employer will be doing. This information is essential so that the occupier employer can:

(a)   be satisfied that the measures put in place by the visiting employer will not only protect visiting employees from exposure to the substances concerned, but also the occupier's employees;

(b)   provide their own employees with information and instruction about any hazardous substances that the visiting employer will be using or the work will produce; and

(c)   reassure their own employees that any exposure to the substances concerned and any risks to their health are being properly controlled.

People working under the control and direction of others

39   Although only the courts can give an authoritative interpretation of the law, in considering the application of COSHH and guidance to people working under another's direction, the following should be considered:

(a)   if people working under the control and direction of others are treated as self-employed for tax and national insurance purposes, they may nevertheless be treated as their employees for health and safety purposes;

(b)   it may, therefore, be necessary to take appropriate action to protect them; and

(c)   if any doubt exists about who is responsible for the health and safety of a worker, this could be clarified and included in the terms of a contract.

40   However, a legal duty under section 3 of the Health and Safety at Work etc Act 1974 (HSW Act)[18] cannot be passed on by the means of a contract and there will still be duties towards others under section 3 of the HSW Act. If such workers are employed on the basis that they are responsible for their own health and safety, legal advice should be sought before doing so.

Duties of employees

41   The main duties of employees are to:

(a)   co-operate with their employers so far as this is necessary to enable employers to meet their obligations under the Regulations, eg by following established procedures which minimise the risk of exposure;

(b)   make full and proper use of control measures including personal protective equipment and report defects (see regulation 8(2));

(c)   ensure that equipment is returned after use to any storage place the employer provides for it, and to report immediately to the employer, ie the 'foreman', supervisor or safety representative as appropriate, any defects discovered in equipment;

(d)   attend, where appropriate, medical examinations at the appointed time and give a medical inspector (formerly known as an employment medical adviser) of the HSE's Employment Medical Advisory Service or appointed doctor information about their health that may reasonably be required (see regulation 11(8)); and

(e)   report any accident or incident which has or may have resulted in the release into the workplace of a biological agent which could cause severe human disease (see regulation 13(5)).

Regulation 4

Regulation

4

Prohibitions relating to certain substances

(1)   Those substances described in Column 1 of Schedule 2 are prohibited to the extent set out in the corresponding entry in Column 2 of that Schedule.

(2)   The importation into the United Kingdom, other than from another member State, of the following substances is prohibited, namely –

(a)   2-naphthylamine, benzidine, 4-aminodiphenyl, 4-nitrodiphenyl, their salts and any substance containing any of those compounds in a total concentration equal to or greater than 0.1 per cent by mass;

(b)   matches made with white phosphorus,

and a contravention of this paragraph shall be punishable under the Customs and Excise Management Act 1979[(a)] and not as a contravention of a health and safety regulation.

(3)   A person shall not supply during the course of or for use at work a substance or article specified in paragraph (2).

(4)   A person shall not supply during the course of or for use at work, benzene or a substance containing benzene unless its intended use is not prohibited by item 11 of Schedule 2.

(a) 1979 c.2.

Exemptions

42   The reference to 'another member State' in regulation 4(2) means the other 24 countries which, with the UK, comprise the European Union. The regulation is required to reflect the principle of free trade within the EU but because the list of prohibited substances implement an EU Directive, the same prohibitions apply in other member States. Therefore, in practice, the exemption in regulation 4(2), ie *'importation … other than from another member State'*, carries no relaxation.

43   HSE can grant exemptions from these prohibitions under regulation 15. However, it can do so only where it would not contravene any requirement imposed by the European Union, and where it could be satisfied that the health of people would not be prejudiced as a consequence.

Application of regulations 6 to 13

(1) Regulations 6 to 13 shall have effect with a view to protecting persons against a risk to their health, whether immediate or delayed, arising from exposure to substances hazardous to health except –

(a) where and to the extent that the following Regulations apply, namely –

(i) the Coal Mines (Respirable Dust) Regulations 1975[(a)],

(ii) the Control of Lead at Work Regulations 2002[(b)],

(iii) the Control of Asbestos at Work Regulations 2002[(c)];

(b) where the substance is hazardous to health solely by virtue of its radioactive, explosive or flammable properties, or solely because it is at a high or low temperature or a high pressure;

(c) where the risk to health is a risk to the health of a person to whom the substance is administered in the course of his medical treatment.

(2) In paragraph (1)(c) "medical treatment" means medical or dental examination or treatment which is conducted by, or under the direction of a –

(a) registered medical practitioner;

(b) registered dentist; or

(c) other person who is an appropriate practitioner for the purposes of section 58 of the Medicines Act 1968[(d)],

and includes any such examination or treatment conducted for the purpose of research.

(a) SI 1975/1433, as amended by SI 1978/807.
(b) SI 2002/2676.
(c) SI 2002/2675.
(d) 1968 c.67.

5

COSHH and DSEAR

44 In accordance with regulation 5(1), COSHH only applies to substances which are hazardous to health. Substances which are capable of producing effects on health as a result of their explosive or flammable properties (an explosion may easily injure a person) are not covered by COSHH, regulation 5(1)(b). Such substances will be subject to the requirements of DSEAR.

45 DSEAR contains wide definitions of the terms 'dangerous substance' and 'explosive atmosphere'. Some substances may also satisfy the definition of a substance hazardous to health in COSHH. For example, certain extremely flammable gases such as hydrogen, methane, propane etc can act as simple asphyxiants and reduce the oxygen content in a workplace to the extent that life cannot be supported and so satisfy the definition of a substance hazardous to health in COSHH. However, the extremely flammable properties of those gases also brings them within the scope of DSEAR. Therefore, where substances with this dual effect are present at the workplace and the work is liable to result in employees being exposed to those substances, employers will have duties under both COSHH and DSEAR to protect the health and safety of their employees.

5

46   In meeting the requirements of both COSHH and DSEAR, employers should consider and adopt the best practical measures for achieving the overall protection of the health and safety of their employees.

Other person who is an appropriate practitioner

47   The reference to 'other person who is an appropriate practitioner' in regulation 5(2)(c) applies to people such as appropriate nurse practitioners, State registered chiropodists, registered midwives, people who hold a certificate of proficiency in ambulance paramedic skills etc who may prescribe certain medicines under the Prescription Only Medicines (Human Use) Order 1997.[19]

Biological agents

48   Three broad categories of exposure to biological agents may be distinguished as:

(a)   exposure resulting from a deliberate intention to work with a biological agent, ie work with biological agents that involves research, development, teaching or diagnosis;

(b)   exposure which arises out of the work activity, but is incidental to it, ie the activity does not involve direct work with the agent itself. Examples of activities in which there may be exposure of this kind are health care, food production, agriculture, refuse disposal and work in sewage purification;

(c)   exposure which does not arise out of the work activity itself, for example where one employee catches a respiratory infection from another.

49   COSHH applies only to the categories of exposure described in (a) and (b) above. This is because regulation 2(2) specifies that COSHH covers only those circumstances where risks of exposure are work related, and not those where they have no direct connection with the work being done.

Regulation 6

Assessment of the risk to health created by work involving substances hazardous to health

(1)   An employer shall not carry out any work which is liable to expose any employees to any substance hazardous to health unless he has –

(a)   made a suitable and sufficient assessment of the risk created by that work to the health of those employees and of the steps that need to be taken to meet the requirements of these Regulations; and

(b)   implemented the steps referred to in sub-paragraph (a).

(2)   The risk assessment shall include consideration of –

(a)   the hazardous properties of the substance;

(b)   information on health effects provided by the supplier, including information contained in any relevant safety data sheet;

(c)   the level, type and duration of exposure;

(d) the circumstances of the work, including the amount of the substance involved;

(e) activities, such as maintenance, where there is the potential for a high level of exposure;

(f) any relevant workplace exposure limit or similar occupational exposure limit;

(g) the effect of preventive and control measures which have been or will be taken in accordance with regulation 7;

(h) the results of relevant health surveillance;

(i) the results of monitoring of exposure in accordance with regulation 10;

(j) in circumstances where the work will involve exposure to more than one substance hazardous to health, the risk presented by exposure to such substances in combination;

(k) the approved classification of any biological agent; and

(l) such additional information as the employer may need in order to complete the risk assessment.

(3) The risk assessment shall be reviewed regularly and forthwith if –

(a) there is reason to suspect that the risk assessment is no longer valid;

(b) there has been a significant change in the work to which the risk assessment relates; or

(c) the results of any monitoring carried out in accordance with regulation 10 shows it to be necessary,

and where, as a result of the review, changes to the risk assessment are required, those changes shall be made.

(4) Where the employer employs 5 or more employees, he shall record –

(a) the significant findings of the risk assessment as soon as is practicable after the risk assessment is made; and

(b) the steps which he has taken to meet the requirements of regulation 7.

The COSHH risk assessment

50 The purpose of the assessment is to enable the employer to make a valid decision about the measures necessary to prevent or adequately control the exposure of their employees to substances hazardous to health arising from the work. It also enables the employer to demonstrate readily, both to themselves and to others who may have an interest, eg safety representatives, enforcement authorities etc that they have:

(a) considered all the factors pertinent to the work;

(b) reached an informed and valid judgement about the risks;

(c) considered the practicability of preventing exposure to hazardous substances;

(d) considered the steps which need to be taken to achieve and maintain adequate control of exposure where prevention is not reasonably practicable in accordance with regulation 7;

(e) considered the need for monitoring exposure at the workplace as part of validating an initial or conditional assessment and for health surveillance; and

(f) identified other action necessary to comply with regulations 8-13.

51 The assessment may be initial or conditional, ie it may prescribe measures that are likely to adequately control exposure, but which need to be tested to confirm their effectiveness. Such measures may subsequently be found to be unnecessary, for example personal protective equipment (PPE) may be provided as a precautionary measures, which is later found not to be required.

52 The COSHH assessment can be made as part of, or as an extension of, the more general risk assessment duties placed on employers by regulation 3 of the Management Regulations.[17] If the substances hazardous to health present in the workplace are also a risk to the safety of employees, eg they are flammable, unstable etc, the employer may find it helpful to combine the COSHH risk assessment with that required by regulation 5 of DSEAR.[11]

Safety data sheets

53 In many circumstances employers will only need to read suppliers' safety data sheets to decide whether their existing practices are sufficient to ensure adequate control of exposure. In other circumstances, and in particular for new activities, employers may need to consult HSE guidance notes, manufacturers' standards, technical papers, trade literature etc to estimate the likely exposure before deciding what control measures they should apply.

54 Employers making an assessment of an activity which exposes employees to a substance (or preparation) which is classified as dangerous for supply under CHIP, must consider and take into account the information the supplier provides on the CHIP safety data sheet (the data sheet). These provide users of dangerous substances with some of the information they need to protect the health of employees and for handling the substance safely in the workplace. The data sheet contains information under a number of obligatory headings, eg 'Hazard identification', 'Exposure controls – personal protection' and so can be a useful source of information in helping employers make the decisions required for the assessment.

55 Accurate, complete and correct information on data sheets is essential when considering workplace controls, eg over-classification of a substance might lead to unnecessarily stringent controls, while under-classification may result in risks to employees' health. If employers have concerns about the quality and reliability of information provided on a data sheet, or if they are unsure of the application of the information to their situation, they should contact the supplier for clarification or for further guidance.

56 The process of carrying out an assessment is not a bureaucratic exercise or simply the collection of information resulting in mountains of paper to be filed away and forgotten. Collecting manufacturers' or suppliers' data sheets and other information does *not* in itself meet the COSHH requirements to carry out an

assessment. Gathering the information is only the first stage in the assessment process. The information must then be used to determine the appropriate control measures needed to protect the health of employees, for example by following the step-by-step approach described in *COSHH essentials*[20,21] (see paragraphs 85 and 103-105).

Biological agents

57   For biological agents, as distinct from other substances hazardous to health, the assessment should reflect the ability they may have to replicate and infect. In general, there will not be a dose-response relationship of the kind that exists for many other substances, and risk may be high at small exposures. Relevant information on the nature of a particular agent includes that prepared by the Advisory Committee on Dangerous Pathogens.

The person who carries out the assessment

58   Employers must ensure that whoever carries out the assessment and provides advice on the prevention and control of exposure is competent to do so in accordance with regulation 12(4). This does not necessarily mean that particular qualifications are required. However, whoever carries out the assessment should:

(a)   have adequate knowledge, training and expertise in understanding hazard and risk (see paragraphs 255-259);

(b)   know how the work activity uses or produces substances hazardous to health;

(c)   have the ability and the authority to collate all the necessary, relevant information; and

(d)   have the knowledge, skills and experience to make the right decisions about the risks and the precautions that are needed.

59   The person who carries out the assessment does not always have to be fully familiar with the requirements of COSHH and the ACOP. However, that person should have access to someone who has a firm grasp of those requirements. This pooling of knowledge would allow, for example, a supervisor's experience of a process to be combined with the technical and legal knowledge of a health and safety manager.

60   If more than one person contributes to the assessment, the employer should ensure that each person knows precisely what they are to do, and nominate one person to co-ordinate, compile and record the significant findings.

Making a suitable and sufficient assessment

61   The assessment should determine whether there are any substances hazardous to health (including biological agents) at the workplace to which employees are liable to be exposed, and in a form in which the substance can be inhaled, ingested or absorbed through the skin.

62   Assessment of the risks created by any work must be comprehensive and cover those items listed in regulation 6(2). It should take into account those substances which are:

(a)   brought into the workplace and handled, stored and used for processing;

(b)   produced or given off, eg as fumes, vapour dust etc by a process or an activity or as a result of an accident or incident;

(c)   used for, or arise from maintenance, cleaning, and repair work;

(d)   produced at the end of any process, eg wastes, residues, scrap etc; and

(e)   produced from activities carried out by another employer's employees in the vicinity.

63   For those hazardous substances brought into and used in the workplace, the employer's first priority is to prevent exposure to the substance by identifying and substituting a non-hazardous or less hazardous alternative. This should be a thorough and comprehensive process:

(a)   in which the employer considers and evaluates the hazards posed by any alternative substances that are available and the degree of risk they may present in the work activity concerned; and

(b)   which results in the employer selecting for use the substance that produces the least risk for the circumstances of the work.

64   Where a substance is a known or suspected carcinogen or mutagen, there is a more compelling reason for the employer to make every effort to substitute a non-carcinogenic or non-mutagenic alternative.

65   The assessment of the risks created by the work activity should also include consideration of:

(a)   the properties, ie physical, chemical or biological of the substances and the effects they could have on the body;

(b)   where those substances are likely to be present and in what form, eg dust, vapour, mist, fume etc and whether they are used or produced, and in what amounts and how often;

(c)   the ways in which and the extent to which any groups of people could be exposed, including maintenance workers who may work in circumstances where exposure is foreseeably higher than normal: office staff, night cleaners, security guards, members of the public such as visitors, patients etc, taking into account the type of work and process, and any reasonably foreseeable deterioration in, or failure of, any control measure provided;

(d)   the need to protect particular groups of employees who may be at an increased risk, eg inexperienced trainees and young people aged under 18; pregnant workers; disabled workers; and any employees known to be susceptible to certain illnesses such as dermatitis, asthma or other diseases which may be caused by exposure to hazardous substances;

(e)   an estimate of exposure, taking into account any information that may be available about:

(i)   the concentration likely to be produced by the work concerned;

(ii)   the effort needed to do the work and how this may affect the rate and volume of air employees breathe (for some work activities, employees might breathe three or four times the volume of air that they would breathe at rest); and

6

(iii) the effect of any engineering measures and systems of work currently used for controlling potential exposure. To complete the assessment, it may be necessary to carry out atmospheric sampling and measurement to determine exposure, particularly where operations are complex or specialised and the substances involved have an occupational exposure limit;

(f) how the estimate of exposure compares with any existing, valid standards which represent adequate control, eg an occupational exposure limit or 'biological monitoring guidance value'.

66 Employers should give particular consideration to activities which can give rise to the highest exposures, eg cleaning of equipment, work in confined spaces, or non-routine or end-of-shift tasks. Understanding the factors that contribute to employees' exposure will help employers decide how to control it.

67 If a comparison of the estimate of exposure with any existing valid standards, which represent adequate control, shows that control is likely to be inadequate then the assessment should also describe the extra steps needed to obtain and maintain adequate control, eg better enclosure and extraction.

Exposure to two or more substances

68 Where a work activity may expose employees to more than one substance hazardous to health, the employer must consider the possible enhanced harmful effects of combined or sequential exposures. If employees are under health surveillance which is being supervised by a doctor or other health professional, the employer should seek advice from the medical person concerned. Otherwise, information may be available from other sources such as the individual suppliers of the substances, trade associations or guidance material etc.

Assessment of the risks from biological agents

69 For exposure to biological agents, the employer should consider in particular:

(a) the hazard groups of any biological agents that may be present and what form they may be in, eg infectious stages or hardy spores;

(b) how and where they are present, how they are transmitted and the diseases they cause; and

(c) the likelihood of exposure and consequent disease (including the identification of workers and non-workers, eg hospital patients, who may be particularly susceptible, for example because they are immunocompromised), drawing on evidence of the prevalence of infection or other ill effect as experienced within a particular industry sector or workplace.

70 In certain circumstances, for example in medical facilities or livestock farming, the assessment should take account of uncertainties about the presence of infectious agents in patients or animals. The risks associated with tissues and other waste material removed from patients and animals, or specimens sent for examination, should be assessed at each stage of handling, for example during clinical care, surgery, biopsy and other specimen collection, specimen handling and transportation, laboratory examination and waste disposal.

6

Using personal protective equipment to secure adequate control of exposure

71   In deciding what measures are needed to control exposure, employers should only use personal protective equipment (PPE) so far as is reasonably practicable after all other measures have been taken. Employers may use PPE as secondary protection in combination with other control methods such as local exhaust ventilation, if those other control measures do not adequately control exposure by themselves. However, there may be circumstances where an employer considers it prudent to issue personal protective equipment such as clothing, face shields, gloves etc, not because other control measures are inadequate on their own, but to provide employees with additional protection should any of those measures fail.

Recording the significant findings

72   All employers must carry out an assessment but those employing five or more employees must also record the significant findings. Although employers with fewer than five employees are exempt from this recording requirement, they are strongly advised to record the significant findings of their assessments as a matter of good practice. Employers can use the recorded findings as evidence:

(a)   to show the enforcing authorities that they have carried out a suitable and sufficient assessment in accordance with regulation 6(1); and

(b)   to demonstrate that they have systematically considered all the factors relevant to the work, and put in place measures either to prevent exposure or to achieve and maintain adequate control of exposure.

73   The significant findings of the risk assessment should represent an effective statement of hazards, risks and actions taken to protect the health of employees and anyone else who may be affected by the work. Employers will need to record sufficient detail of the assessment itself so that they can demonstrate to a safety representative or inspector etc that they have carried out a suitable and sufficient assessment. The record may refer to and rely on other documents and records describing procedures and safeguards.

74   The record may be in writing or recorded by other means, eg electronically so long as it is readily accessible and retrievable at any reasonable time for use by employers in reviews or for examination, eg by a safety representative or inspector etc.

75   The amount of information employers should record will be proportionate to the risks posed by the work. In the simplest and most obvious cases where a work activity involving exposure to a hazardous substance poses little or no risk, eg for many of the substances often found in small quantities in offices or homes, the employer need only record:

(a)   the substances to which the employees are or are likely to be exposed and the form in which they occur – liquid, powder, pellets, dust etc;

(b)   the measures taken under regulation 7 to adequately control exposure, eg taking account of the information provided by the supplier, and using the substances in accordance with their accompanying instructions; and

(c)   a statement that because the substances pose little or no risk, no further detailed risk assessment is necessary.

76   Where exposure to a number of different hazardous substances pose little or no risk to the health of employees, the employer may group together on a single record the significant findings of the assessments for all the individual substances concerned. The record may also group together the significant findings for similar substances of low risk, eg lubricants or detergents.

77   However, where the work concerned presents more of a risk to health, the significant findings of the assessment should comprise a more comprehensive record. It should include at least the appropriate items from the following list:

(a)   the processes or activities in which the substances are used or produced and how employees may be exposed to them;

(b)   the substance(s) to which the employees are liable to be exposed and the form in which it/they occur, eg liquid, gas, vapour, powder;

(c)   the hazards and risks the substances present under normal conditions of use, and in circumstances of an unforeseen incident, accident or emergency which could result in an uncontrolled release of the substance concerned into the workplace;

(d)   the extent to which prevention and substitution of a substance or process was considered (see regulations 7(1)(2));

(e)   identification of the employees or groups of employees liable to be exposed;

(f)   the preventive measures in place to achieve adequate control of exposure, including the use of any personal and respiratory protective equipment (RPE). (These need not duplicate details of measures more fully described in other documents such as standard operating procedures but could refer to them);

(g)   the commissioning, monitoring and testing required as part of the process of validating the effectiveness of and refining control measures;

(h)   whether it is necessary to carry out atmospheric sampling and measurement and the frequency with which any further air monitoring will be carried out;

(i)   where appropriate, the reasons for selecting particular types of PPE, including where appropriate RPE, to secure adequate control of exposure;

(j)   the conclusions reached on the risks to the health of employees and to any other people who may be affected by the work concerned, taking account of the control measures being used;

(k)   whether it is appropriate to place any identified groups of employees under health surveillance (regulation 11);

(l)   when the assessment will be reviewed or the period between successive reviews.

78   This record of the significant findings will also form the basis for a revision of the assessment.

When to record the significant findings

79   The employer should record the significant findings when the assessment is made or as soon as is practicable afterwards. In some circumstances, not all the significant findings will have been determined at the same time: some may be awaiting further information before they can be resolved and it will not be possible to record these until then, eg air monitoring results. In these situations, the employer should complete or update the significant findings as soon as the information becomes available. However, the employer must ensure that while waiting for information to confirm the conclusions drawn from the assessment, a cautious approach is adopted to ensure that employees' exposure to substances hazardous to health is adequately controlled, eg in emergency situations where operational decisions have to be made and remedial action taken immediately, or in circumstances where there is a pilot operation which must be run for a period before being assessed completely.

Reviewing the assessment

80   The record of the assessment should be a living document, which must be revisited to ensure that it is kept up to date. The employer should make arrangements to ensure that the assessment is reviewed regularly. The date of the first review and the length of time between successive reviews will depend on the type of risk, the work and the employer's judgement on the likelihood of changes occurring.

81   The assessment should be reviewed immediately:

(a)   when there is evidence to think that it may no longer be valid, for example from:

   (i)   the results of examinations and tests of engineering controls (regulation 9);

   (ii)   the results of monitoring exposure (regulation 10);

   (iii) the results of health surveillance, eg the identification of an adverse health effect or a confirmed case of work-related disease (regulation 11(9)); or new information on health risks; or

   (iv)   reports or complaints from supervisors, safety representatives or employees about defects in the control systems;

(b)   where there is to be or has been a significant change in the circumstances of work, especially one which may have affected employees' exposure to a substance hazardous to health. For example:

   (i)   a change in the substances used, including the introduction of a substitute substance, or their source;

   (ii)   in plant modification, including engineering controls;

   (iii) a process or method of work which is likely to affect the nature of the hazard, eg changes in the exhaust ventilation system;

   (iv)   in the volume or rate of production; or

6

(v)   a reduction in the workforce without any corresponding reduction in the rate of production and the consequential additional pressures on employees.

82   Where the assessment is changed and control measures changed or adapted to meet the new circumstances, employers must take action to implement any necessary changes identified by the review and record afresh the significant findings.

83   When reviewing the assessment, employers should use the opportunity to look again at their prevention or control measures. In particular, they should:

(a)   reconsider whether it is practicable to prevent exposure to hazardous substances by changing the process or by using a non-hazardous substance. This may be possible because of technological developments, or changes in the relationship between costs and substances, equipment used and control measures;

(b)   reconsider whether it is practicable to use a less hazardous form of the same substance;

(c)   re-examine existing control measures to decide whether they can be improved.

Consulting employees and their representatives

84   Employers should involve their employees, and/or their safety representatives where they are appointed, in the processes of carrying out and reviewing risk assessments. They are in a good position to know what happens in practice and they will use the controls that the employer introduces. Employers can involve their employees as part of their duties under regulation 12 of COSHH to provide them with suitable information, instruction and training. Employers should also:

(a)   tell employees or their workplace representatives the results of the assessment;

(b)   explain how control measures are designed to protect their health from substances hazardous to health; and

(c)   explain how any changes will affect the way the employees do the work in the future.

Help with the risk assessment

COSHH essentials

85   The HSC's Advisory Committee on Toxic Substances has developed *COSHH essentials*[20,21] as a generic risk assessment scheme for a wide range of hazardous substances covered by CHIP and COSHH. It leads users to appropriate control advice for a range of common tasks, eg mixing, weighing, spray painting (see paragraphs 103-105). *COSHH essentials* is available both in printed and electronic (web-based) formats, and can be used as a basis for the recording of the risk assessment. While *COSHH essentials* has been designed to ensure that a precautionary approach is taken towards control, it is a generic guide and cannot guarantee that in all circumstances it will lead to full compliance with the Regulations' assessment and control requirements. At present, *COSHH essentials* addresses risks from some of the more hazardous substances, eg some substances

that cause asthma or cancer (and it will cover more of these in the future). For those substances not covered, *COSHH essentials* recommends users seek specialist advice. Details are contained in the publication *COSHH essentials: Easy steps to control chemicals*.[20] The electronic *COSHH essentials* can be found at www.coshh-essentials.org.uk.[20]

Other sources of help

86   HSE's publication *A step by step guide to COSHH assessment*[22] provides more general guidance on the stages in carrying out COSHH risk assessments.

87   Some industries, trade associations, industry advisory councils, health departments and professional bodies etc produce guidance publications setting out COSHH-related best practice for the industry concerned. Employers may find these other publications helpful in carrying out their assessments.

88   Employers who decide to use the services of a consultancy to carry out their assessment(s), or to design and check the effectiveness of control measures should ensure that they are competent to do the work. One way to do this is to use one listed in the British Institute of Occupational Hygienists (BIOH) Directory of Consultancies. Contact BIOH at Suite 2, Georgian House, Great Northern Road, Derby DE1 1LT Tel: 01332 298087 Website: www.bioh.org.uk.

6

Regulation 7

Prevention or control of exposure to substances hazardous to health

Regulation

(1)   Every employer shall ensure that the exposure of his employees to substances hazardous to health is either prevented or, where this is not reasonably practicable, adequately controlled.

(2)   In complying with his duty of prevention under paragraph (1), substitution shall by preference be undertaken, whereby the employer shall avoid, so far as is reasonably practicable, the use of a substance hazardous to health at the workplace by replacing it with a substance or process which, under the conditions of its use, either eliminates or reduces the risk to the health of his employees.

(3)   Where it is not reasonably practicable to prevent exposure to a substance hazardous to health, the employer shall comply with his duty of control under paragraph (1) by applying protection measures appropriate to the activity and consistent with the risk assessment, including in order of priority –

(a)   the design and use of appropriate work processes, systems and engineering controls and the provision and use of suitable work equipment and materials;

(b)   the control of exposure at source, including adequate ventilation systems and appropriate organisational measures; and

(c)   where adequate control of exposure cannot be achieved by other means, the provision of suitable personal protective equipment in addition to the measures required by sub-paragraphs (a) and (b).

(4)   The measures referred to in paragraph (3) shall include –

(a)   arrangements for the safe handling, storage and transport of substances

7

hazardous to health, and of waste containing such substances, at the workplace;

(b) *the adoption of suitable maintenance procedures;*

(c) *reducing, to the minimum required for the work concerned –*

    (i) *the number of employees subject to the exposure,*

    (ii) *the level and duration of exposure, and*

    (iii) *the quantity of substances hazardous to health present at the workplace;*

(d) *the control of the working environment, including appropriate general ventilation; and*

(e) *appropriate hygiene measures including adequate washing facilities.*

(5) *Without prejudice to the generality of paragraph (1), where it is not reasonably practicable to prevent exposure to a carcinogen or mutagen, the employer shall apply the following measures in addition to those required by paragraph (3) –*

(a) *totally enclosing the process and handling systems, unless this is not reasonably practicable;*

(b) *the prohibition of eating, drinking and smoking in areas that may be contaminated by carcinogens or mutagens;*

(c) *cleaning floors, walls and other surfaces at regular intervals and whenever necessary;*

(d) *designating those areas and installations which may be contaminated by carcinogens or mutagens and using suitable and sufficient warning signs; and*

(e) *storing, handling and disposing of carcinogens or mutagens safely, including using closed and clearly labelled containers.*

(6) *Without prejudice to the generality of paragraph (1), where it is not reasonably practicable to prevent exposure to a biological agent, the employer shall apply the following measures in addition to those required by paragraph (3) –*

(a) *displaying suitable and sufficient warning signs, including the biohazard signs shown in Part IV of Schedule 3;*

(b) *specifying appropriate decontamination and disinfection procedures;*

(c) *instituting means for the safe collection, storage and disposal of contaminated waste, including the use of secure and identifiable containers, after suitable treatment where appropriate;*

(d) *testing, where it is necessary and technically possible, for the presence, outside the primary physical confinement, of biological agents used at work;*

(e) specifying procedures for working with, and transporting at the workplace, a biological agent or material that may contain such an agent;

(f) where appropriate, making available effective vaccines for those employees who are not already immune to the biological agent to which they are exposed or are liable to be exposed;

(g) instituting hygiene measures compatible with the aim of preventing or reducing the accidental transfer or release of a biological agent from the workplace, including –

   (i) the provision of appropriate and adequate washing and toilet facilities, and

   (ii) where appropriate, the prohibition of eating, drinking, smoking and the application of cosmetics in working areas where there is a risk of contamination by biological agents; and

(h) where there are human patients or animals which are, or are suspected of being, infected with a Group 3 or 4 biological agent, the employer shall select the most suitable control and containment measures from those listed in Part II of Schedule 3 with a view to controlling adequately the risk of infection.

(7)   Without prejudice to the generality of paragraph (1), where there is exposure to a substance hazardous to health, control of that exposure shall only be treated as being adequate if -

(a) the principles of good practice for the control of exposure to substances hazardous to health set out in Schedule 2A are applied;

(b) any workplace exposure limit approved for the substance is not exceeded; and

(c) for a substance –

   (i) which carries the risk phrase R45, R46 or R49, or for a substance or process which is listed in Schedule 1; or

   (ii) which carries the risk phrase R42 or R42/43, or which is listed in section C of HSE publication "Asthmagen? Critical assessments of the evidence for agents implicated in occupational asthma" as updated from time to time, or any other substance which the risk assessment has shown to be a potential cause of occupational asthma, exposure is reduced to as low a level as is reasonably practicable.

(9)   Personal protective equipment provided by an employer in accordance with this regulation shall be suitable for the purpose and shall –

(a) comply with any provision in the Personal Protective Equipment Regulations 2002[(a)] which is applicable to that item of personal protective equipment; or

7

(a) SI 2002/1144.

(b)   in the case of respiratory protective equipment, where no provision referred to in sub-paragraph (a) applies, be of a type approved or shall conform to a standard approved, in either case, by the Executive.

(10) Without prejudice to the provisions of this regulation, Schedule 3 shall have effect in relation to work with biological agents.

(11) In this regulation, "adequate" means adequate having regard only to the nature of the substance and the nature and degree of exposure to substances hazardous to health and "adequately" shall be construed accordingly.

Prevention of exposure

89   An employer's overriding duty and first priority is to consider how to prevent employees being exposed to substances hazardous to health by all routes (regulation 7(1) and 7(2)). Employers who do not first consider this are failing to comply with a fundamental requirement of the Regulations. The duty to prevent exposure should be achieved by measures other than the use of personal protective equipment. Employers can best comply with this requirement by eliminating completely the use or production of substances hazardous to health in the workplace. This might be achieved by:

(a)   changing the method of work so that the operation giving rise to the exposure is no longer necessary; or

(b)   modifying a process to eliminate the production of a hazardous by-product or waste product; or

(c)   substituting wherever reasonably practicable, a non-hazardous substance which presents no risk to health where a hazardous substance is used intentionally.

90   In many workplaces, it will not be possible or practicable to eliminate exposure to substances hazardous to health completely. Therefore, where it is necessary to use a hazardous substance, an employer should consider whether it is possible to reduce exposure and risk to the health of employees significantly by using:

(a)   an alternative less hazardous substance; or

(b)   a different form of the same substance; or

(c)   a different process.

For example, by changing the form of the substance concerned so that exposure is negligible, eg using a substance in pellet rather than powder form.

91   Among the factors an employer will need to take into account when considering an alternative substance are the harmful properties of any proposed replacement. The harmful properties of many potential replacement substances may not all be known. Care should be taken when there are gaps in the knowledge about the potential of the substance to cause harm. The ultimate decision should be based on a balance of any new risks they might present against the potential benefits. For example, an employer's choice of a replacement substance with lower toxicity but higher flammability might increase the overall risk if the process has an intrinsic fire risk. In considering potential substitutes, employers should be aware of the responsibilities they have under other regulations, eg DSEAR.

92   More guidance on substitution is provided by HSE's publication *Seven steps to successful substitution of hazardous substances.*[23]

Adequate control of exposure

93   Where prevention of exposure to substances hazardous to health is not reasonably practicable, employers must comply with the secondary duty in regulation 7(1) to control exposure adequately by all routes. To achieve this, employers must consider and apply, where appropriate for the circumstances of the work:

(a)   the measures set out in regulation 7(3) in the priority order given;

(b)   the specific measures in regulation 7(4);

(c)   the principles of good practice for the control of exposure to substances hazardous to health set out in Schedule 2A, as required by regulation 7(7)(a) (see paragraphs 295-357 for guidance on the principles);

(d)   ensure, in accordance with regulation 7(7)(b), that any WEL approved for a substance hazardous to health is not exceeded (see regulation 10); and

(e)   reduce exposure so far as is reasonably practicable for:

   (i)   a substance which carries the risk phrase R45, R46 or R49, or for a substance or process which is listed in Schedule 1; or

   (ii)   a substance which carries the risk phrase R42 or R42/43, or which is listed in section C of the HSE publication *Asthmagen? Critical assessments of the evidence for agents implicated in occupational asthma,*[24] or any other substance which the risk assessment has shown to be a potential cause of occupational asthma.

94   The employer should apply the principles of good practice (see paragraphs 295-357) in all circumstances, but it will not always be necessary to apply all the controls described in regulation 7(3) and (4). A combination of them will often be necessary to best protect the health of employees. The employer should give priority to those controls that contain or minimise the release of contaminants and the spread of hazardous substances into the workplace.

95   The administrative and procedural options for control are also important elements that the employer should consider, eg the arrangements for the safe handling, storage and transport of hazardous substances, of waste containing such substances, and suitable maintenance procedures etc.

96   The specific standards that are needed to achieve adequate control of exposure by each route of exposure, ie inhalation, absorption through the skin and ingestion, are described in paragraphs 120-141.

Specific control measures

97   Regulation 7(4) supports regulation 7(3) by providing a list of typical control measures that employers should apply if indicated as necessary in the risk assessment. The objective is to use the findings of the risk assessment to select the control measure or the combination of control measures that are proportionate to the risk and which will achieve adequate control of exposure.

98 Appropriate application of the principles of good practice for the control of exposure to substances hazardous to health will enable employers to select the optimum combination of control measures which may include:

(a) totally enclosed process and handling systems;

(b) plant or process changes which, for instance:

    (i) keep the production or generation of the hazardous dust, fume, vapour, biological agent etc to a minimum, eg by modifying a process or changing its conditions such as temperature or pressure to reduce emissions,

    (ii) contain hazardous substances within the plant,

    (iii) reduce or eliminate the need for maintenance staff to go into hazardous areas, and

    (iv) limit the area contaminated if spills and leaks occur;

(c) changes to systems of work which, for instance:

    (i) identify and define methods of work which minimise emission, generation or release of substances hazardous to health,

    (ii) reduce people's exposure time,

    (iii) minimise the number of people exposed;

(d) ventilation:

    (i) partial enclosure, with local exhaust ventilation,

    (ii) local exhaust ventilation, and/or

    (iii) sufficient general ventilation;

further guidance is available from the HSE publications HSG37 *An introduction to local exhaust ventilation*,[25] and HSG202 *General ventilation in the workplace*;[26]

(e) reducing to the minimum required for the work:

    (i) the number of employees exposed and excluding non-essential employees, eg by using 'refuges',

    (ii) the level and duration of exposure, and

    (iii) the quantities of hazardous substances used or produced;

(f) regular cleaning of contamination from walls, surfaces etc or their disinfection;

(g) providing safe handling, storage, transport and disposal of substances hazardous to health and waste containing such substances;

(h) hygiene measures:

(b) Health and safety professionals

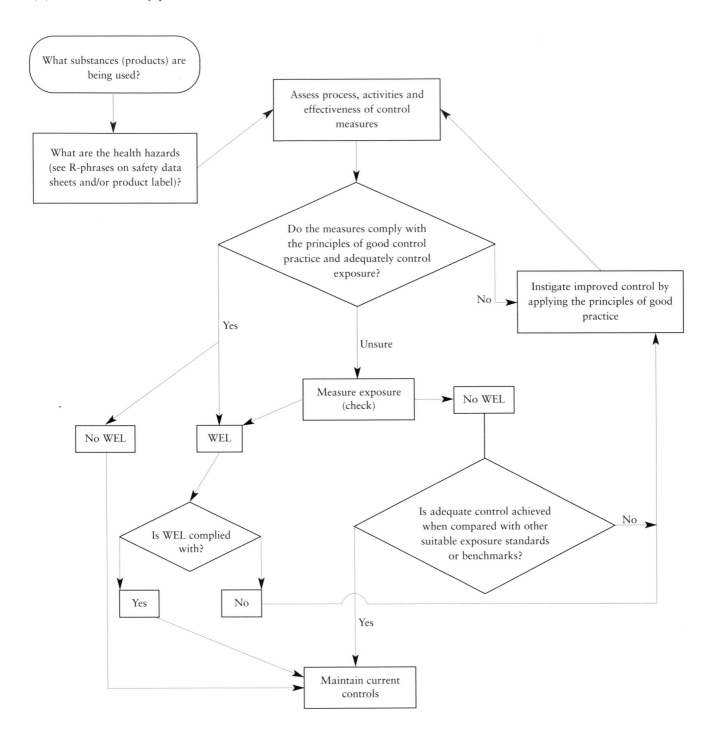

Control of exposure to carcinogens and mutagens

107 If it is not reasonably practicable to prevent exposure to a carcinogen or mutagen (substances assigned one of the risk phrases R45, R46 or R49 (see paragraph 93(e)), or listed in Schedule 1, the employer must put into place the appropriate controls set out in regulation 7(3) and all the measures in regulation 7(5). This means that whether or not it is reasonably practicable to enclose totally the process and handling systems in accordance with regulation 7(5)(a), all the other measures in 7(5)(b)-(e) are still required.

108 Further guidance on the control of exposure to carcinogens and mutagens is set out in Appendix 1.

Control of exposure to substances that cause occupational asthma

109 Additional ACOP duties on the control of substances that cause occupational asthma are set out in Appendix 3. A list of substances that can cause occupational asthma is available on the HSE website at www.hse.gov.uk/asthma/causes/htm.

Further general guidance

110 The HSE publication *EH40/2005 Workplace exposure limits*:[26]

(a) provides a list of those hazardous substances for which HSC has approved a WEL;

(b) gives the details of the limit(s) concerned;

(c) lists the risk phrases from CHIP for the WELs;

(d) identifies substances with WELs that are also defined as carcinogens, mutagens or substances that can cause occupational asthma for the purposes of COSHH;

(e) lists the appropriate control approach under *COSHH essentials*;[20,21] and

(f) provides further helpful guidance, eg work activities which may result in exposure to the substance concerned.

Control of exposure to biological agents

111 If employers cannot prevent exposure to a biological agent they should take steps to ensure that it is controlled adequately and consider all the requirements set out in regulation 7(3), (4), (6) and (7). They should apply the principles of good practice and use each requirement where, and to the extent that:

(a) it is applicable; and

(b) the assessment carried out under regulation 6 shows that it will lead to a reduction in risk.

112 The selection of control measures for biological agents should take into account the fact that there are no exposure limits for them. Their ability to replicate and to infect at very small doses means that exposure may have to be reduced to levels that are at the limit of detection.

113 Not all the listed measures will be required in every case. The assessment may indicate for example that:

(a) a specific method of transmission and route of infection is required;

(b) a susceptible host is needed;

(c) there is a low prevalence of the infection in that particular activity; and

(d) illness is treatable easily leading to rapid and complete recovery.

Other substances assigned a WEL

128 For a substance assigned a WEL that is not classified under COSHH as a carcinogen, mutagen or a cause of occupational asthma adequate control of exposure will be achieved by applying the principles of good practice to the work involving exposure to the substance concerned and keeping the exposure below any WEL.

Inhaled substances not assigned WELs

129 The absence of a substance from the lists of WELs does not mean that it is safe. Many substances do not have a WEL. For these substances, employers should apply the principles of good practice for the control of substances hazardous to health to control exposure to a level to which nearly all the working population could be exposed, day after day at work, without adverse effects on health. HSE has published good practice advice to help employers decide on suitable control measures. Available material includes the guidance on Schedule 2A (see paragraphs 295-357), *COSHH essentials*[20,21] (see paragraphs 103-105), process - specific guidance for a number of common processes and Chemical Hazard Alert Notices (CHANs).[28] A list of CHANs and other HSE guidance currently available can be viewed on the HSE website at www.hse.gov.uk/pubns. In addition, employers can obtain information about the substance concerned from a number of other sources, including:

(a) manufacturers and suppliers of the substance;

(b) industry associations; and

(c) occupational medicine and occupational hygiene journals.

130 If it is not possible to identify suitable exposure control measures using, for instance, *COSHH essentials* and no WEL exists it may be possible and useful to identify or develop an exposure standard. Suppliers, trade associations or specialist advisers may be able to help.

Action if an occupational exposure limit is exceeded

131 A WEL or other exposure standard should not normally be exceeded. If it is, the employer should check the continuing effectiveness of the control measures. There may be something obviously wrong which can be corrected. If the reasons for the excessive exposure are not obvious, a more detailed investigation may be needed. This could involve task-based 'and process-related measurements to identify when and why raised exposures are occurring. Employers who are unsure of the implications of results that exceed a WEL, or other exposure standard, should obtain appropriate advice from an expert', such as an occupational hygienist.

132 If the employer concludes that the exposure monitoring results do not indicate adequate control of exposure, the further steps to take should include:

(a) checking control measures to ensure that they are working as they should. For instance that exhaust ventilation is performing to design specification or people are following the defined methods of working which are necessary to minimise their exposure;

(b) liaising with managers, safety representatives and employees to check that all the principles of good practiceare being applied correctly, and to establish possible reasons for the rise in the measured exposure to the substance concerned;

(c) considering whether it is necessary to provide the employees who may be exposed to the substance concerned with suitable RPE. This should be a temporary measure only until the situation is returned to normal and adequate control of exposure is re-established;

(d) devising and implementing a programme of immediate action to reinforce the control measures where a WEL is exceeded and particularlyso where the substance concerned is a carcinogen, mutagen or a cause of occupational asthma; and

(e) making further measurements of exposure in order to check that any remedial action to tighten control has been effective.

133 If further exposure measurements raise doubts as to whether adequate control is being achieved, the employer should review the assessment to decide whether additional and more effective controls are needed.

134 For detailed advice on the sampling strategies suitable for measuring exposure and practical guidance on interpreting the results in relation to occupational exposure limits, see HSE's publication *Monitoring strategies for toxic substances*.[29]

Adequate control of exposure by routes other than inhalation

135 COSHH requires that employers prevent or control exposure adequately by all routes, not just the inhalation route, and deals with substances which can be hazardous to health by:

(a) absorption through the skin or mucous membranes; or

(b) contact with the skin or mucous membranes, eg dermatitis, chemical burns and microbial infection; or

(c) ingestion.

136 HSE's publication *EH40/2005 Workplace exposure limits*[27] (see paragraph 110) lists those substances that have been assigned a WEL and which can be absorbed through the skin to a significant extent and identifies them with a skin (Sk) notation. Safety data sheets and hazard warning labels are other useful sources of information about substances that have the potential to affect and be absorbed through the skin.

Absorption through the skin

137 In handling any substance which has been assigned an 'Sk' notation, the employer's application of good practice controls, work methods and other precautionary measures should prevent the substance coming into contact with the employee's skin. Employers should also prepare a contingency plan to deal with incidents where a substance makes contact with an employee's skin. The plan should draw on any information and advice provided by the supplier on the particular characteristics and properties of the substance and how to deal with spillages etc.

(d)   the environment in which it will be worn; and

(e)   in dusty environments, whether the materials selected reduce the tendency for dust to collect on the PPE and be re-released.

147   Manufacturers of PPE must ensure that their products comply with the Personal Protective Equipment Regulations 2002.[32]

Suitable RPE

148   For each work activity for which it is foreseen that employees will need to wear RPE, the employer should specify the suitable equipment to be worn to make sure that employees are given adequate protection. To be suitable, RPE must be capable of controlling adequately the inhalation exposure using as a guide the equipment's assigned protection factor as listed in HSE publication *The selection, use and maintenance of respiratory protective equipment: A practical guide.*[33] The selection and provision of suitable RPE should be based on a range of considerations:

(a)   the level of protection claimed by manufacturers for different types of RPE, and identification of those types that will provide a greater degree of protection than that required for likely or known exposure;

(b)   the type of work to be done; the physical effort required to do it; the length of time the equipment will have to be worn; the requirements for visibility, comfort and the need for employees to communicate with each other; its compatibility with any other PPE that may be needed (for example, safety glasses);

(c)   the different facial characteristics of the RPE wearers, to ensure that the equipment fits correctly, and is matched to the wearer. In addition the equipment must be matched to the job and the environment in which it is to be used. The selection of suitable equipment should be undertaken in full consultation with the wearers. This will help to ensure that the wearers have the most comfortable equipment best suited for them and which, as a consequence, is likely to be the most effective in use;

(d)   it must be 'CE' marked if it was manufactured on or after 1 July 1995 to show that it is manufactured to meet minimum legal requirements. However, where RPE was manufactured before 1 July 1995 then it must either be 'CE'-marked or HSE-approved;

(e)   employees should be trained properly in its use and supervised;

(f)   it should be cleaned and checked regularly to ensure that it remains effective.

Fit testing of facepieces

149   The performance of RPE with a tight-fitting facepiece (filtering facepieces, half and full-face masks) depends on a good contact between the wearer's skin and the face seal of the mask. A good face seal can only be achieved if the wearer is clean shaven in the region of the seal and the facepiece is of the correct size and shape to fit the wearer's face. If spectacles with side arms and other PPE are also worn, they should not interfere with the correct fitting of the facepiece or the face seal. The performance of RPE with a loose-fitting facepiece, eg visors, helmets, hoods etc, is less dependent on a tight fit on the face, but nevertheless requires the correct size to ensure the wearer achieves an adequate fit and protection.

150 Employers should ensure that the selected facepiece (tight and loose-fitting types) is of the right size and can correctly fit each wearer. For a tight-fitting facepiece (filtering facepieces usually known as disposable masks, half and full-face masks) the initial selection should include fit testing to ensure the wearer has the correct device. The test will assess the fit by determining the degree of face-seal leakage of a test agent while the RPE user is wearing the facepiece under test. For full-face masks, a suitable quantitative fit test should be used and the pass level fit factor is 2000. For devices such as filtering facepieces and half masks, the pass level fit factor is 100. For these lower performance facepieces, a suitable and validated qualitative method (often called a semi-quantitative test) can be carried out instead. Employers must ensure that whoever carries out the fit testing is competent to do so in accordance with regulation 12(4).

151 Repeat fit testing will be needed when changing to a different model of RPE or a different sized facepiece or if there have been significant changes to the facial characteristics of the individual wearer, eg as a result of significant weight gain or weight loss or due to dentistry. Repeat fit testing will not be required following a change of employer, provided that the same model of RPE continues to be used by the employee.

152 The quantitative fit testing may be carried out using:

(a)   a test chamber which uses a salt aerosol or sulphur hexafluoride gas to assess the face-seal leakage;

(b)   a portable device at the workplace which measures particulates in air to assess the face-seal leakage; or

(c)   a portable device at the workplace which measures pressure variations inside the facepieces to assess the face-seal leakage.

153 Qualitative test methods use bitter or sweet-tasting aerosols. When the tests are carried out, the facepiece wearer will perform simple exercises as indicated by the competent person carrying out the test. More information on the selection, including information on assigned protection factors, use and fit testing of RPE is contained in the HSE publications, *The selection, use and maintenance of respiratory protective equipment: A practical guide*[33] and *Fit testing of respiratory protective equipment facepieces.*[34]

Facilities for washing, changing, eating and drinking

154 Employers should provide certain facilities to:

(a)   ensure that employees meet and maintain a standard of personal hygiene that is consistent with adequate control of exposure;

(b)   avoid the spread of substances hazardous to health; and

(c)   reduce the risk of ingestion of substances hazardous to health.

155 The facilities include:

(a)   *adequate washing facilities.* These should be sited in a convenient position but situated so that they do not themselves become contaminated. The facilities provided should relate to the type and level of exposure;

(iii)   there are valid techniques for detecting indications of the disease or effect,

and the technique of investigation is of low risk to the employee.

(3)   The employer shall ensure that a health record, containing particulars approved by the Executive, in respect of each of his employees to whom paragraph (1) applies, is made and maintained and that that record or a copy thereof is kept available in a suitable form for at least 40 years from the date of the last entry made in it.

(4)   The employer shall –

(a)   on reasonable notice being given, allow an employee access to his personal health record;

(b)   provide the Executive with copies of such health records as the Executive may require; and

(c)   if he ceases to trade, notify the Executive forthwith in writing and make available to the Executive all health records kept by him.

(5)   If an employee is exposed to a substance specified in Schedule 6 and is engaged in a process specified therein, the health surveillance required under paragraph (1) shall include medical surveillance under the supervision of a relevant doctor at intervals of not more than 12 months or at such shorter intervals as the relevant doctor may require.

(6)   Where an employee is subject to medical surveillance in accordance with paragraph (5) and a relevant doctor has certified by an entry in the health record of that employee that in his professional opinion that employee should not be engaged in work which exposes him to that substance or that he should only be so engaged under conditions specified in the record, the employer shall not permit the employee to be engaged in such work except in accordance with the conditions, if any, specified in the health record, unless that entry has been cancelled by a relevant doctor.

(7)   Where an employee is subject to medical surveillance in accordance with paragraph (5) and a relevant doctor has certified by an entry in his health record that medical surveillance should be continued after his exposure to that substance has ceased, the employer shall ensure that the medical surveillance of that employee is continued in accordance with that entry while he is employed by the employer, unless that entry has been cancelled by a relevant doctor.

(8)   An employee to whom this regulation applies shall, when required by his employer and at the cost of the employer, present himself during his working hours for such health surveillance procedures as may be required for the purposes of paragraph (1) and, in the case of an employee who is subject to medical surveillance in accordance with paragraph (5), shall furnish the relevant doctor with such information concerning his health as the relevant doctor may reasonably require.

(9)   Where, as a result of health surveillance, an employee is found to have an identifiable disease or adverse health effect which is considered by a relevant doctor or other occupational health professional to be the result of exposure to a substance hazardous to health the employer of that employee shall –

(a)   ensure that a suitably qualified person informs the employee accordingly and provides the employee with information and advice regarding further health surveillance;

(b)   review the risk assessment;

(c)   review any measure taken to comply with regulation 7, taking into account any advice given by a relevant doctor, occupational health professional or by the Executive;

(d)   consider assigning the employee to alternative work where there is no risk of further exposure to that substance, taking into account any advice given by a relevant doctor or occupational health professional; and

(e)   provide for a review of the health of any other employee who has been similarly exposed, including a medical examination where such an examination is recommended by a relevant doctor, occupational health professional or by the Executive.

(10)   Where, for the purpose of carrying out his functions under these Regulations, a relevant doctor requires to inspect any workplace or any record kept for the purposes of these Regulations, the employer shall permit him to do so.

(11)   Where an employee or an employer is aggrieved by a decision recorded in the health record by a relevant doctor to suspend an employee from work which exposes him to a substance hazardous to health (or to impose conditions on such work), he may, by an application in writing to the Executive within 28 days of the date on which he was notified of the decision, apply for that decision to be reviewed in accordance with a procedure approved for the purposes of this paragraph by the Health and Safety Commission, and the result of that review shall be notified to the employee and employer and entered in the health record in accordance with the approved procedure.

The objectives of health surveillance

214   The objectives of health surveillance are to:

(a)   protect the health of individual employees by detecting as early as possible adverse changes which may be caused by exposure to substances hazardous to health;

(b)   help evaluate the measures taken to control exposure;

(c)   collect, keep up to date and use data and information for determining and evaluating hazards to health.

215   Assessing employees' immunity before or after vaccination will provide an indication of their fitness to work with that particular biological agent, as required by the Management Regulations. Routine testing for antibodies or the taking of specimens to attempt to isolate infectious agents is not generally appropriate, unless there is an indication that infection may have occurred. If an employee is found to be suffering from an infection or illness which is suspected to be the result of exposure at work, other employees who have been similarly exposed should be placed under suitable surveillance until it is established that they are not affected. Where there are early symptoms of disease that employees themselves may be able to recognise, an effective measure is to provide instruction and information that will enable them to do so, and systems for symptom reporting. This, though, is not 'health surveillance' within the strict meaning of the Regulations.

216 The results of health surveillance, and particularly any adverse results, should lead to some action which will benefit employees' health. Therefore, before health surveillance takes place, the employer should decide:

(a)   the options and criteria for action; and

(b)   the method of recording, analysing and interpreting the results.

Suitable health surveillance

217 Suitable health surveillance will *always* include the keeping of an individual health record (see paragraphs 235-239). There are a number of health surveillance procedures which can be used. The most suitable one will depend on the particular workplace circumstances. The range of available procedures includes the following:

(a)   *biological monitoring* is the measurement and assessment of workplace agents or their metabolites (substances formed when the body converts the chemical) in exposed workers. Measurements are made either on samples of breath, urine or blood, or any combination of these. This may be appropriate where it is possible to link the results directly to an adverse health effect, eg mercury, cadmium;

(b)   *biological effect monitoring* is the measurement and assessment of early biological effects in exposed workers caused by absorption of chemicals;

(c)   *medical surveillance*, ie both health surveillance under the supervision of a medical inspector of the HSE's Employment Medical Advisory Service, or an appointed doctor for the purpose of regulation 11(5) and under the supervision of a registered medical practitioner. It may include clinical examinations and measurements of physiological, eg lung function testing and the psychological effects of exposure to hazardous substances in the workplace which may show as changes or alterations in body function;

(d)   *enquiries* about symptoms, inspection or examination by a suitably qualified person, eg an occupational health nurse;

(e)   *inspection* by a responsible person such as a supervisor or manager, eg for chrome ulceration;

(f)   *review of records and occupational history* during and after exposure; this should check the correctness of the assessment of risks to health and indicate whether the assessment should be reviewed.

218 The different types of procedures need not be independent of each other because the results of one might indicate the need for another. For example the results of biological monitoring may show a need for other health surveillance procedures.

The person who carries out health surveillance procedures

219 For employees exposed to a substance specified in Schedule 6 and working in the related listed process, regulation 11(5) specifies the frequency of medical surveillance carried out under the supervision of medical inspectors or appointed doctors. This is at intervals not exceeding 12 months, or at such shorter intervals as the medical inspector or appointed doctor requires, and the exact nature of the examination is at their direction and discretion.

220 Other health surveillance procedures should be carried out either under the supervision of a registered medical practitioner or, where appropriate, by a suitably qualified person, eg an occupational health nurse or a responsible person. A responsible person is someone appointed by the employer who is competent, in accordance with regulation 12(4), to carry out the relevant procedure and who is charged with reporting to the employer the conclusions of the procedure.

When health surveillance is appropriate

221 Health surveillance, including medical surveillance under the supervision of a medical inspector or appointed doctor, is appropriate for employees liable to be exposed to the substances and working in the processes listed in Schedule 6 if the specific conditions laid down in regulation 11(2)(a) apply. Health surveillance, including the keeping of health records, will also be appropriate when employees are exposed to hazardous substances and the three requirements of regulation 11(2)(b) are satisfied.

222 The judgements that employers make under regulation 11(2)(a) and (b) on the likelihood that an identifiable disease or adverse health effect will result from or may be related to exposure should:

(a)   relate to the type and extent of exposure;

(b)   include assessment of current scientific knowledge such as:

    (i)   available epidemiology;

    (ii)   information on human exposure;

    (iii) human and animal toxicological data; and

    (iv)   extrapolation from information about similar substances or situations.

223 Valid health surveillance techniques need to be sufficiently sensitive and specific to detect abnormalities related to the type and level of exposure concerned. Those carrying out the health surveillance should know how to interpret data and this may mean having to identify normal values and to set action levels. The aim should be to establish health surveillance procedures which are easy to perform, preferably non-invasive and acceptable to employees. In particular, procedures should be safe, that is of low risk to workers. None should be carried out if there is a risk of an employee's health being harmed.

224 Health surveillance procedures may need to be reviewed, modified or discontinued, as appropriate, depending on which of the criteria set out in paragraphs 222-223 can be applied to the particular work conditions and exposures concerned.

225 Table 2 gives examples where health surveillance is appropriate under the criteria in regulation 11(2)(b) together with information on typical forms of surveillance. The list is not definitive and there will be other instances where health surveillance is required under the criteria at 11(2)(b).

Table 2 Substances for which health surveillance is appropriate under regulation 11(2)(b)

Substance/process			Typical procedure
(a)		Substances of recognised systemic toxicity (ie substances that can be breathed in, absorbed through the skin or swallowed and that affect parts of the body other than where they enter).	Appropriate clinical or laboratory investigations. Biological effect monitoring.
(b)		Substances known to cause occupational asthma.	Enquiries seeking evidence of respiratory symptoms related to work.
(c)		Substances known to cause severe dermatitis.	Skin inspection by a responsible person.
(d)	(i)	Electrolytic plating or oxidation of metal articles by use of an electrolyte containing chromic acid or other chromium compounds.	Skin inspection by a responsible person.
	(ii)	Contact with chrome solutions in dyeing processes using dichromate of potassium or sodium.	
	(iii)	Contact with chrome solutions in processes of liming and tanning of raw hides and skins (including re-tanning of tanned hides or skins).	

226 Other examples of where it is appropriate to carry out health surveillance are provided in relevant technical literature including HSE Guidance Notes.

Detection of an adverse health effect or identifiable disease

227 Where an employee is found to have an adverse health effect or identifiable disease which a medical inspector, appointed doctor or other occupational health professional considers to be the result of exposure to a substance hazardous to health, the employer must arrange for the employee concerned to be interviewed and told.

228 The employer should consult the medical inspector, appointed doctor or occupational health professional concerned to consider:

(a) whether it is necessary to transfer the employee to other work where there is no exposure to the hazardous substance concerned;

(b) whether a medical examination of the employee concerned should be arranged and if so, the person who should carry it out;

(c) if a medical examination is necessary, whether all other employees who have been similarly exposed to the substance concerned as the affected employee should also be medically examined; and

(d) if necessary, the facilities which should be provided and the arrangements which should be made.

229 Taking into account any advice received from the medical inspector etc, the employer must also ensure that the employee who has suffered the adverse health effect or identifiable disease is advised by a suitably qualified person of the:

(a) arrangements which will be put in place for continuing health surveillance;

(b) arrangements, if any, to transfer the employee to alternative employment within the workplace; and

(c) action to be taken to reassess the workplace controls.

230 The employee concerned should also be advised to visit their own doctor (general practitioner) to report the ill-health condition so that the doctor is aware of the work the employee does, and the adverse health effect which has resulted from exposure to the substance(s) concerned.

231 Any adverse health effects or identifiable diseases resulting from exposure to a substance hazardous to health should automatically prompt the employer to:

(a) review the assessment of the work in accordance with regulation 11(9)(b); and

(b) where necessary, review and revise the control measures in place to prevent a recurrence of the ill-health effect or disease.

Continuing health surveillance after exposure has ceased

232 In certain circumstances it may be appropriate for an employer to continue health surveillance of their employees (at least while they remain their employees) after exposure to a substance hazardous to health has ceased. The circumstances where this will benefit workers may be those where an adverse effect on health may be anticipated after a latent period and where it is believed that the effect can be reliably detected at a sufficiently early stage. Examples might include those substances which cause cancer of the urinary tract.

Facilities for health surveillance

233 Where health surveillance procedures are carried out at the employer's premises, suitable facilities should be available. Where the nature of the examinations or inspections requires it, the facilities should include a room which is:

(a) clean, warm and well-ventilated;

(b) suitably furnished with a table and seats;

(c) equipped with a washbasin with hot and cold running water, soap and a clean towel. If it is not reasonably practicable to provide hot and cold running water, either a supply of warm water should be provided or the means of heating water in the room;

(d) set aside for the exclusive purpose of health and safety when required and it should provide privacy.

234 Where a substantial number of employees is to be examined or assessed, the employer should also provide a suitable waiting area when reasonably practicable. Where employees are providing specimens for biological monitoring or biological effect monitoring, an adjacent toilet with hand-washing facilities should be available.

Health records

235 Employers must keep an up-to-date health record for each individual employee placed under health surveillance. It should contain at least the following particulars which are approved by HSE:

(a) identifying details:

    (i) surname;

    (ii) forenames;

    (iii) gender;

    (iv) date of birth;

    (v) permanent address and post code;

    (vi) National Insurance number;

    (vii) date when present employment started; and

    (viii) a historical record of jobs in this employment involving exposure to identified substances requiring health surveillance;

(b) results of all other health surveillance procedures and the date on which and by whom they were carried out. The conclusions should relate *only* to the employee's fitness for work and will include, where appropriate:

    (i) a record of the decisions of the medical inspector or appointed doctor; or

    (ii) conclusions of the medical practitioner, occupational health nurse or other suitably qualified or responsible person.

236 The health record should not include confidential clinical data. In accordance with regulation 11(3), employers must keep these health records for at least 40 years. They may be kept in any format, eg on paper or electronically. Where records are kept electronically, employers should ensure that they have a suitable back-up system that allows access to copies of the records in the event of a serious computer failure.

When individual health records only are required

237 In some circumstances, the only health surveillance required is the setting up and maintenance of individual health records containing the information in paragraph 235(a). Examples are:

(a) known or suspected carcinogens except those in Schedule 6 shown in Table 2 (see paragraph 225);

(b) machine-made mineral fibres, also known as 'man-made' mineral fibres and MMMF;

(c) rubber manufacturing and processing giving rise to rubber process dust and rubber fume (except the entry for indiarubber in Schedule 6);

(d) leather dust in boot and shoe manufacture, arising during preparation and finishing.

238 Where health surveillance consists only of setting up and maintaining an individual health record, the information required is that in paragraph 235(a).

239 In addition to keeping the particulars in paragraph 235, the employer should also keep an index or list of the names of people undergoing, or who have undergone, health surveillance. The record should be kept in a form compatible with and capable of being linked to those required by regulation 10 for monitoring of exposure, so that, where appropriate, the type and extent of exposure can be compared with effects. For example, where personal exposure monitoring under regulation 10 is carried out for an employee who is under health surveillance in accordance with regulation 11, the employer may keep the information required by regulations 10(6) and 11(3) on the same record.

Disposing of records when a business ceases to trade

240 When an employee or employer's representative, eg an appointed administrator, receiver or liquidator, decides that the business will cease trading, the employer should contact a medical inspector at the HSE area office nearest to where the business is located, and offer to provide the employees' health records (or copies of them) for safe keeping.

Access to employees' records

241 As well as allowing their employees to see their own individual health records maintained under regulation 11(3), employers may, with the employee's consent, also allow the employee's representatives to see them. Where, under regulation 11(4)(b), HSE requests copies of an employee's personal health records, the employer should provide the information summarised in paragraph 235.

11

Regulation 12

Information, instruction and training for persons who may be exposed to substances hazardous to health

(1) Every employer who undertakes work which is liable to expose an employee to a substance hazardous to health shall provide that employee with suitable and sufficient information, instruction and training.

(2) Without prejudice to the generality of paragraph (1), the information, instruction and training provided under that paragraph shall include –

(a) details of the substances hazardous to health to which the employee is liable to be exposed including –

(i) the names of those substances and the risk which they present to health,

(ii) any relevant workplace exposure limit or similar occupational exposure limit,

12

(iii)   access to any relevant safety data sheet, and

(iv)   other legislative provisions which concern the hazardous properties of those substances;

(b)   the significant findings of the risk assessment;

(c)   the appropriate precautions and actions to be taken by the employee in order to safeguard himself and other employees at the workplace;

(d)   the results of any monitoring of exposure in accordance with regulation 10 and, in particular, in the case of a substance hazardous to health for which a workplace exposure limit has been approved, the employee or his representatives shall be informed forthwith, if the results of such monitoring show that the workplace exposure limit has been exceeded;

(e)   the collective results of any health surveillance undertaken in accordance with regulation 11 in a form calculated to prevent those results from being identified as relating to a particular person; and

(f)   where employees are working with a Group 4 biological agent or material that may contain such an agent, the provision of written instructions and, if appropriate, the display of notices which outline the procedures for handling such an agent or material.

(3)   The information, instruction and training required by paragraph (1) shall be –

(a)   adapted to take account of significant changes in the type of work carried out or methods of work used by the employer; and

(b)   provided in a manner appropriate to the level, type and duration of exposure identified by the risk assessment.

(4)   Every employer shall ensure that any person (whether or not his employee) who carries out work in connection with the employer's duties under these Regulations has suitable and sufficient information, instruction and training.

(5)   Where containers and pipes for substances hazardous to health used at work are not marked in accordance with any relevant legislation listed in Schedule 7, the employer shall, without prejudice to any derogations provided for in that legislation, ensure that the contents of those containers and pipes, together with the nature of those contents and any associated hazards, are clearly identifiable.

Suitable and sufficient information, instruction and training

242 In addition to the list in regulation 12(2), the information provided to employees and to other people on the premises should include where appropriate:

(a)   the purpose of health surveillance, the duty of employees to attend for health surveillance procedures on the appointed date and time, and arrangements for employees to have access to their individual health records (see regulation 11(4)(a) and (8));

(b)   when to use the hygiene facilities provided and the importance of doing so in accordance with agreed procedures;

(c)   any further relevant information resulting from a review of the assessment: why it has been done and how any changes will affect the way employees do the work in the future;

(d)   any procedures for dealing with accidents, incidents and emergencies prepared in accordance with regulation 13. Employers should ensure that all employees have the opportunity to read and discuss the procedures with their safety representatives.

243   Regulation 12(2)(a)(iii) allows employees, including safety representatives who are employees, access to any relevant safety data sheet. These sheets are not always the best or most appropriate way of providing employees with information about the risks associated with the use of hazardous substances in the workplace. Employers may instead choose to distil the information from safety data sheets onto more readable and understandable in-house information and training documents. In doing so, employers should take every care in transcribing the information and in amplifying warnings and precautions accurately. While this is an acceptable practice, employees and their safety representatives must still be allowed access to safety data sheets relevant to the work should they want to see them.

244   The other legislative provisions referred to in regulation 12(2)(a)(iv) are those that apply directly to the hazardous substances to which employees are liable to be exposed. These may include, for example, CHIP[5]; the Control of Pesticides Regulations 1986 (as amended);[38] and DSEAR[11] for those substances which may also have a flammable, oxidising or explosive property.

245   Where workers are exposed to Hazard Group 4 biological agents, the employer must provide written instructions setting out the procedures for handling the agent.

246   If the nature of the workplace and the activity are such that workers may need instant access to this information, then it should be set out on notices displayed in the workplace.

247   The extent of the information, instruction and training will vary with the complexity of the hazards, risks, processes and controls that the risk assessment will identify. Employers should aim to strike a balance between providing sufficient information for an employee to carry out work safely, and providing too much information that may result in overburdening and confusing the employee. So where, for example, a substance is being used that is not particularly hazardous and exposure is adequately controlled, basic instructions and training may be all that is required.

248   Employers have a duty under the Management Regulations[17] to ensure that the information they provide is comprehensible. Therefore, they should consider all the various ways of providing information, instruction and training and select those most appropriate to their own circumstances. The range of options includes: class or group tuition, individual tuition, written instructions including leaflets, courses etc. Employers should also decide how much time is needed to provide suitable and sufficient training etc for their employees to comply fully with the requirements of the Management Regulations. New employees should be provided with proper induction training which should always cover emergency and evacuation procedures.

Updating information

249   Providing information, instruction and training is not a one-off exercise. Information, instruction and training should be reviewed and updated whenever significant changes are made to the type of work carried out or to the work methods used. Significant changes might include the amount of substances used or produced, new control measures, new substances brought into the workplace, automation of certain processes. Further information and training following a review of the assessment should cover why the assessment was reviewed, any changes to the way the work is to be done and the precautions the employees should take to protect themselves and others.

Making information available to safety representatives

250 The employer must make all relevant information available to employees or their representatives in accordance with the Health and Safety (Consultation with Employees) Regulations 1996,[39] and the Safety Representatives and Safety Committees Regulations 1977.[40]

Instruction and training

251 The instruction and training must ensure that people at work on the premises do not put themselves, or others at risk through exposure to substances hazardous to health. In particular, the instruction must be sufficient and suitable for them to know:

(a) how and when to use the control measures;

(b) the defined methods of work;

(c) how to use the personal protective equipment and especially respiratory protective equipment, eg the correct method of removing and refitting gloves and masks and determining how long protective gloves should be worn before any liquid contamination is liable to permeate them;

(d) the cleaning, storage and disposal procedures they should follow, why they are required and when they are to be carried out, eg cleaning contaminated PPE with water or a vacuum fitted with a high-efficiency particulate arrester (HEPA) filter, and not with an airline, or the risks of using contaminated PPE;

(e) the procedures to be followed in an emergency.

252 Training should include elements of theory as well as practice. Training in the use and application of control measures and PPE should take account of recommendations and instructions supplied by the manufacturer.

12

Records of training

253 Employers may find it helpful to keep a record of the training given to individual employees or specific groups of named employees. The records may provide a useful checklist for ensuring that employees receive all the necessary training etc at the appropriate time. The records may also help to resolve any disputes that arise about whether the employer has provided a particular employee with a specific aspect of information, instruction and training.

Providing employees with copies of their records

254 As a matter of good practice, employers should offer to make available to employees copies of any monitoring or health surveillance records which relate to them personally when their employment ends for any reason. The employer should advise the employee to keep the records indefinitely in a secure place.

12

People carrying out work on behalf of the employer

255 The employer must ensure that the person, or people, to whom any work is delegated is qualified to do it and this may mean having to use the services of consultants and outside experts. If this becomes necessary, the employer will still need to ensure that the people engaged receive sufficient information about the

12

particular circumstances of the work, including the hazardous substances used or produced and their hazardous properties.

256 Employers have duties under the Management Regulations to appoint one or more competent persons to assist them in carrying out the measures needed to comply with health and safety legislation. The Management Regulations further require that where the employer has an employee with the necessary competence to provide the required assistance, the employer should appoint the employee to do the work in preference to someone who is not in their employment. Wherever practicable, therefore, suitable employees should be encouraged to have appropriate training, and to gain the knowledge and expertise that will give them the competence to help their employers comply with health and safety requirements.

257 People carrying out the work required under regulations 6, 7 and 10 of COSHH should have adequate knowledge, training and expertise in the assessment, evaluation and control of risks arising from exposure to substances hazardous to health. The British Institute of Occupational Hygienists (BIOH) is the professional body in the UK widely recognised for its occupational hygiene qualifications. It sets and maintains benchmarks of competence in occupational hygiene practice. The Institute sets courses and examinations with levels of competence which range from introductory short courses to full professional certification.

258 Where a degree of formal training is required, the BIOH has devised modules based on one-week training courses followed by examination eg, modules on 'Health effects of hazardous substances'; 'Measurement of hazardous substances' (including COSHH assessments); and 'Control of hazardous substances'. A shorter, two- to three-day module, 'COSHH', is also available for those requiring a brief introduction to COSHH. Certificates of competence are awarded to individuals who pass both the written examination and oral examination on some modules. BIOH modules are run by many different organisations across the country with practical experience of implementing the various requirements of COSHH. A list of course dates, venues and the names of the organisations which have organised courses is available from BIOH.

259 For more complex situations expert advice may be appropriate. HSE does not define or approve standards of competence, but those seeking expert advice may wish to consult a professional occupational hygienist. The BIOH maintains a register of competent practitioners. For the address and telephone number of BIOH, see paragraph 88.

Identifying the contents of containers and pipes

260 Regulation 12(5) is intended to cover those circumstances where there is no other legal requirement for employers to identify the hazardous contents of containers and pipes. These legal requirements, which implement European Directives, are listed in Schedule 7.

261 Many containers will therefore already be adequately marked with their contents because of supply requirements. Similarly, pipework is often marked in accordance with BS 1710: 1984 *Specification for identification of pipelines and services*[41] or equivalent 'in-house' standards. However, there are containers and pipes whose contents are not individually marked because it is not practicable to do so, eg the pipework at large petrochemical complexes whose content may change frequently during the course of a process or operation.

be used should be made with regard to the level and type of risk, and a worst case estimate of the likely concentration of a hazardous substance in the air in the workplace;

(e) *first-aid facilities* sufficient to deal with an incident until the emergency services arrive; where the facilities are located and stored; the likely effects on the workforce of the accident, incident or emergency, eg burns, scalds, shock, the effects of smoke inhalation etc. Employers should note that they have duties to provide first-aid facilities under the Health and Safety (First Aid) Regulations 1981;[43]

(f) *the role, responsibilities and authority* of the people nominated to manage the accident, incident or emergency and the individuals with specific duties in the event of an incident, eg the people responsible for: checking that specific areas have been evacuated; shutting down plant that might otherwise compound the danger; contacting and liaison with the emergency services on their arrival and making sure that they are aware of the hazardous substance(s) that are the cause of or are affected by the emergency;

(g) *procedures for employees* to follow and who should know; how they should respond to an incident and what action they should take; the people who have been assigned specific responsibilities and their roles;

(h) *procedures for clearing up and safely disposing* of any substance hazardous to health damaged or 'contaminated' during the incident;

(i) *regular safety drills*: the frequency of practising emergency procedures will depend on the complexity of the layout of the workplace, the activities carried out, the level of risk, the size of the workforce, the amount of substances involved, and the success of each test;

(j) the special needs of any disabled employees, eg assigning other employees to help them leave the workplace in an emergency.

273 The extended procedures should be compiled in consultation with safety representatives, employees and with those people assigned roles and responsibilities during any emergency.

Incidents involving carcinogens and mutagens

274 If an incident results in the uncontrolled release of a carcinogen or mutagen into the workplace, the equipment the employer provides in accordance with regulation 13(3)(b) must always include suitable respiratory protective equipment, which is capable of providing adequate control of exposure to the carcinogenic or mutagenic substance concerned.

Suitable warning and communication systems

275 Employers must provide suitable communication systems for warning employees who are liable to be affected by an accident, incident or emergency involving substances hazardous to health. The communication system the employer provides will be proportionate to the size of the workplace and workforce, the quantity of substances hazardous to health in the workplace, and the level and type of risk the substances present. The employer may consider it appropriate to provide warning signals for different purposes, ie one type of alarm to warn employees of the need to be prepared to evacuate because an incident is declared, and another signalling the immediate need to evacuate the premises.

13

Suitable warning systems might comprise:

(a)   a continuous or intermittent ringing bell, whistle or hooter;

(b)   warning lights;

(c)   an intercom or a public address system.

276   Employers must ensure that all warning systems can be heard and/or seen in all parts of the premises, and in particular by employees who may work in noisier areas. Employers should also ensure that they take due account of the special needs of disabled employees.

Reviewing the emergency procedures

277   The employer should review, update and replace the emergency procedures in the light of changing circumstances, eg a significant increase in the use of a particularly hazardous substance, changes in the workplace activities involving the use of a new substance hazardous to health etc.

Making procedures available to the emergency services

278   Employers should ensure that copies of their emergency arrangements and procedures are made available to the relevant internal and external accident and emergency services.

Internal emergency services

279   Internal services include those people assigned specific duties in the event of an accident, incident or emergency, eg people responsible for closing down processes or activities where safe to do so; or with liaising with the emergency services on their arrival at the workplace; or safety representatives, first aiders etc. Employers should arrange for all the people concerned to be provided with their own copy of the emergency procedures. Copies may be provided on paper or electronically.

280   Copies of the procedures should be circulated and seen by all employees at least once every six months.

External emergency services

281   Employers who need to extend their emergency procedures to cover situations involving substances hazardous to health should consider whether it is necessary to make all branches of the emergency service aware of their arrangements to deal with accidents and incidents. As a minimum requirement, the employer should contact their local fire service and offer to make available a copy of the business's emergency procedures and the collated information on which they are based.

282   The employer's procedures, including details of the substances hazardous to health present at the workplace, will help the fire service to prepare its own response procedures and precautionary measures if an emergency is declared at the employer's workplace. These measures will ensure that the fire service deals with any declared incident effectively, and especially those likely to occur outside normal working hours, in a way that presents the minimum risk to their own staff.

283 If an incident could have serious repercussions on the environment, the employer should consider whether to make a copy of the business's emergency procedures available to the nearest office of the Environment Agency.

284 A record of the procedures may be kept in writing or recorded by other means, eg electronically. It must be kept readily accessible and retrievable for examination at any reasonable time, eg by a safety representative, inspector etc.

Displaying emergency procedures

285 Where it is appropriate to do so, employers should display the emergency procedures in a prominent position in the workplace for employees to read, eg on employee notice boards. It will be appropriate, for example, where:

(a) the company is fairly small and employees are encouraged to consult their notice board(s) frequently for information about the business and its activities;

(b) the emergency procedures are reasonably short and simple, can be read easily and quickly and can comfortably fit on the notice board.

286 Where an accident or incident could result in the release of a biological agent, it will be appropriate to display the procedures where the employer concludes that:

(a) the type of biological agent present in the workplace, eg a biological agent in Hazard Group 3 or 4 which can cause severe human disease, and the activities concerned, such as working with large volumes of a biological agent, are such that the employees would need to have instant access to emergency procedures to help contain an accidental release; or

(b) by having the emergency procedures constantly and prominently displayed, it is more likely to reduce the risk of an accidental release of a biological agent occurring.

Employer's actions during an emergency

287 The specific actions an employer must take if an accident, incident or emergency occurs are set out in regulation 13(3). Where the incident involves the uncontrolled release of a hazardous substance into the workplace, the employer must exclude all people not concerned with the emergency action from the area of contamination. The employer must ensure that those employees given the task of identifying the source of the release and making repairs wear appropriate personal protective equipment, including, where necessary, suitable respiratory protective equipment and protective clothing with which they have been provided until the situation is restored to normal.

288 As well as telling employees the cause of the incident and the measures taken or to be taken to resolve it, the employer should also ensure that:

(a) any important lessons learned from it are passed onto the employees and/or their appointed safety representatives; and

(b) the information is used in any subsequent review of the risk assessment for the process or activity concerned.

Guidance

13

289 When an incident is declared, employers also have a duty to tell, and if necessary evacuate, other people who are present in the workplace and who may be affected by it. This includes visitors, employees of another employer etc. Employers whose activities involve the presence of certain listed dangerous substances at the workplace also have a duty under COMAH[42] to take all measures necessary to prevent major accidents and to limit their consequences to people and the environment.

ACOP

13

The employee's duty to report the release of certain biological agents

290 An employee must report immediately to their employer or any of their employer's other employees with specific responsibility for health and safety, any accident or incident which results in the release of a biological agent in Hazard Groups 3 or 4. Biological agents in those hazardous groups can cause severe human disease. The training of employees working with such biological agents should prepare them for this responsibility. The training should include highlighting the readily foreseeable incidents that could occur and the procedures for dealing with accidents, incidents and emergencies, and the name of the person or people to whom accidents should be reported.

Regulation 14

Provisions relating to certain fumigations

Regulation

14

(1) This regulation shall apply to fumigations in which the fumigant used or intended to be used is hydrogen cyanide, phosphine or methyl bromide, except that paragraph (2) shall not apply to fumigations using the fumigant specified in Column 1 of Schedule 8 when the nature of the fumigation is that specified in the corresponding entry in Column 2 of that Schedule.

(2) An employer shall not undertake fumigation to which this regulation applies unless he has –

(a) notified the persons specified in Part I of Schedule 9 of his intention to undertake the fumigation; and

(b) provided to those persons the information specified in Part II of that Schedule,

at least 24 hours in advance, or such shorter time in advance, as the persons required to be notified may agree.

(3) An employer who undertakes a fumigation to which this regulation applies shall ensure that, before the fumigant is released, suitable warning notices have been affixed at all points of reasonable access to the premises or to those parts of the premises in which the fumigation is to be carried out and that after the fumigation has been completed, and the premises are safe to enter, those warning notices are removed.

Guidance

14

291 Schedule 8 to the Regulations lists a number of fumigations exempted from the notification requirements of regulation 14. For all three specified gases, these exemptions include fumigations carried out for research and also fumigation in fumigation chambers.

Regulation 15

Regulation

15

Exemption certificates

(1)   Subject to paragraph (2) the Executive may, by a certificate in writing, exempt any person or class of persons or any substance or class of substances from all or any of the requirements or prohibitions imposed by regulation 4 (to the extent permitted by article 9 of Council Directive 98/24/EC), 8, 9, 11(8), (10) and (11) and 14 of these Regulations and any such exemption may be granted subject to conditions and to a limit of time and may be revoked by a certificate in writing at any time.

(2)   The Executive shall not grant any such exemption unless having regard to the circumstances of the case and, in particular, to –

(a)   the conditions, if any, which it proposes to attach to the exemption; and

(b)   any requirements imposed by or under any enactments which apply to the case,

it is satisfied that the health and safety of persons who are likely to be affected by the exemption will not be prejudiced in consequence of it.

Regulation 16

Regulation

16

Exemptions relating to the Ministry of Defence etc

(1)   In this regulation –

(a)   "Her Majesty's Forces" means any of the naval, military or air forces of the Crown, whether raised inside our outside the United Kingdom and whether any such force is a regular, auxiliary or reserve force, and includes any civilian employed by those forces;

(b)   "visiting force" has the same meaning as it does for the purposes of any provision of Part I of the Visiting Forces Act 1952[a]; and

(c)   "headquarters" means a headquarters for the time being specified in Schedule 2 to the Visiting Forces and International Headquarters (Application of Law) Order 1999[b].

(2)   The Secretary of State for Defence may, in the interests of national security, by a certificate in writing exempt –

(a)   any of Her Majesty's Forces;

(b)   any visiting force;

(c)   members of a visiting force working in or attached to a headquarters; or

(d)   any person engaged in work involving substances hazardous to health, if that person is under the direct supervision of a representative of the Secretary of State for Defence,

(a) 1952 c.67.
(b) SI 1999/1736.

from all or any of the requirements or prohibitions imposed by these Regulations and any such exemption may be granted subject to conditions and to a limit of time and may be revoked at any time by a certificate in writing, except that, where any such exemption is granted, suitable arrangements shall be made for the assessment of the health risk created by the work involving substances hazardous to health and for adequately controlling the exposure to those substances of persons to whom the exemption relates.

(3)   Regulation 11(11) shall not apply in relation to –

(a)   any visiting force; or

(b)   members of a visiting force working in or attached to a headquarters.

292 The Secretary of State for Defence has the power to exempt only in the interests of national security. That is, when the state is under threat or otherwise facing an emergency. Exemptions, if needed, should be in writing and would be issued, after consultation with the HSE, for specific activities and for a limited period only. When an exemption is granted, suitable arrangements should still be made to assess the risk to health from the work and for adequately controlling the exposure.

293 A person under the direct supervision of a representative of the Secretary of State for Defence is an employee of the Ministry of Defence (MOD) or a member of Her Majesty's Forces. It also includes certain people employed on Ministry of Defence premises. For example people on a labour-only contract, but whether or not there is direct supervision will depend on the type of contract. People employed on the premises of defence contractors are most unlikely to be under such direct supervision. For example Ministry of Defence liaison staff at a defence contractor's premises do not normally exercise direct supervision.

Regulation 17

Regulation 17 Extension outside Great Britain

(1)   Subject to paragraph (2), these Regulations shall apply to and in relation to any activity outside Great Britain to which sections 1 to 59 and 80 to 82 of the 1974 Act apply by virtue of the Health and Safety at Work etc Act 1974 (Application outside Great Britain) Order 2001(a) as those provisions apply within Great Britain.(a)

(2)   These Regulations shall not extend to Northern Ireland except insofar as they relate to imports of substances and articles referred to in regulation 4(2) into the United Kingdom.

(a) SI 2001/2127.

294 This regulation applies COSHH to offshore installations, wells, pipelines and pipeline works, and to connected activities within the territorial waters of Great Britain or in designated areas of the United Kingdom Continental Shelf, plus certain other activities within territorial waters.

Prohibition of certain substances hazardous to health for certain purposes

Regulation 4(1)

Column 1 Description of substance		Column 2 Purpose for which the substance is prohibited	
1 2-naphthylamine; benzidine; 4-aminodiphenyl; 4-nitrodiphenyl; their salts and any substance containing any of those compounds, in a total concentration equal to or greater than 0.1 per cent by mass.		Manufacture and use for all purposes including any manufacturing process in which a substance described in Column 1 of this item is formed.	
2 Sand or other substance containing free silica.		Use as an abrasive for blasting articles in any blasting apparatus.	
3 A substance –		Use as a parting material in connection with the making of metal castings.	
	(a)	Containing compounds of silicon calculated as silica to the extent of more than 3 per cent by weight of dry material, other than natural sand, zirconium silicate (zircon), calcined china clay, calcined aluminous fireclay, sillimanite, calcined or fused alumina, olivine; or		
	(b)	Composed of or containing dust or other matter deposited from a fettling or blasting process.		
4 Carbon disulphide.		Use in the cold-cure process of vulcanising in the proofing of cloth with rubber.	
5 Oils other than white oil, or oil of entirely animal or vegetable origin or entirely of mixed animal and vegetable origin.		Use for oiling the spindles of self-acting mules.	
6 Ground or powdered flint or quartz other than natural sand.		Use in relation to the manufacture or decoration of pottery for the following purposes:	
		(a)	the placing of ware for the biscuit fire;
		(b)	the polishing of ware;
		(c)	as the ingredient of a wash for saggars, trucks, bats, cranks, or other articles used in supporting ware during firing; and
		(d)	as dusting or supporting powder in potters' shops.

Column 1 *Description of substance*		Column 2 *Purpose for which the substance is prohibited*		
7 Ground or powdered flint or quartz other than –		*Use in relation to the manufacture or decoration of pottery for any purpose except -*		
(a)	*natural sand; or*	*(a)*	*use in a separate room or building for –*	
(b)	*ground or powdered flint or quartz which forms parts of a slop or paste.*		*(i)*	*the manufacture of powdered flint or quartz, or*
			(ii)	*the making of frits or glazes or the making of colours or coloured slips for the decoration of pottery;*
		(b)	*use for the incorporation of the substance into the body of ware in an enclosure in which no person is employed and which is constructed and ventilated to prevent the escape of dust.*	
8 Dust or powder of a refractory material containing not less than 80 per cent of silica other than natural sand.		*Use for sprinkling the moulds of silica bricks, namely bricks or other articles composed of refractory material and containing not less than 80 per cent of silica.*		
9 White phosphorus.		*Use in the manufacture of matches.*		
10 Hydrogen cyanide.		*Use in fumigation except when -*		
		(a)	*released from an inert material in which hydrogen cyanide is absorbed;*	
		(b)	*generated from a gassing powder; or*	
		(c)	*applied from a cylinder through suitable piping and applicators other than for fumigation in the open air to control or kill mammal pests.*	
11 Benzene and any substance containing benzene in a concentration equal to or greater than 0.1 per cent by mass, other than –		*Use for all purposes except -*		
(a)	*motor fuels covered by Council Directive 85/210/EEC (OJ No L96, 3.4.85, p.25);*	*(a)*	*use in industrial processes; and*	
(b)	*waste covered by Council Directives 75/442/EEC (OJ No L194, 25.7.75, p.39), as amended by Council Directive 91/156/EEC (OJ No L78, 26.3.91, p32), and 91/689/EEC (OJ No L377, 31.12.91, p20).*	*(b)*	*for the purposes of research and development or for the purpose of analysis.*	

Schedule 2A

Principles of good practice for the control of exposure to substances hazardous to health

Regulation 7(7)

(a)	Design and operate processes and activities to minimise emission, release and spread of substances hazardous to health.
(b)	Take into account all relevant routes of exposure – inhalation, skin absorption and ingestion – when developing control measures.
(c)	Control exposure by measures that are proportionate to the health risk.
(d)	Choose the most effective and reliable control options which minimise the escape and spread of substances hazardous to health.
(e)	Where adequate control of exposure cannot be achieved by other means, provide, in combination with other control measures, suitable personal protective equipment.
(f)	Check and review regularly all elements of control measures for their continuing effectiveness.
(g)	Inform and train all employees on the hazards and risks from the substances with which they work and the use of control measures developed to minimise the risks.
(h)	Ensure that the introduction of control measures does not increase the overall risk to health and safety.

Principles of good practice

295 The objective of COSHH is to prevent, or adequately control, exposures to substances hazardous to health so as to prevent ill health. This guidance on good practice for the control of exposure to substances hazardous to health is to help employers after they have considered the overriding duty in regulation 7(1) to prevent exposure.

296 Employers have a responsibility to manage and minimise the risks from work activities. They must develop suitable and sufficient control measures and ways of maintaining them. They should:

(a) identify hazards and potentially significant risks;

(b) take action to prevent and control risks; and

(c) keep control measures under regular review.

297 To be effective in the long-term, control measures must be practical, workable and sustainable.

298 Good practice in the control of substances hazardous to health can be encapsulated in eight generic principles. They must all be applied to obtain effective and reliable control. The principles overlap in their application. They are not rank ordered; the first is not more important than the last, although there is a logic to their overall order of presentation. The following guidance explains how to apply the principles in practice.

Principle (a). Design and operate processes and activities to minimise emission, release and spread of substances hazardous to health

299 It is more effective, and usually cheaper, to reduce the emission of a contaminant at source, rather than to develop ways of removing the contaminant from the workplace, once it has been released and dispersed. Sources of exposure should be reduced in number, size, emission or release rate, as much as possible. It is often not possible to obtain adequate and reliable control unless this is done. Both the processes and procedures need to be considered. To identify how people get exposed during work activities, it is essential to recognise the principal sources and how the contaminant is transferred within the workplace. It is easy to miss significant sources and causes of exposure.

300 Processes and activities can lead to the emission and release of contaminants. The way they do this and the scale of emission and release needs to be understood. Once this assessment is available, alterations can be developed to minimise emissions, release and spread of contaminants. It is best to do this at the design stage, but it may well be possible to make useful and relatively low-cost changes to existing processes. Identify and control the worst sources first. In practice, improvements to production and quality can often be useful additional benefits from such re-examinations.

301 People working near a process may be significantly exposed even though those directly involved are protected, for example by wearing PPE. In these circumstances, the most practical option may be to segregate the process. It may be the only viable way to protect those people not directly involved in the process or activity.

302 Once the number and size of sources have been minimised, consider reducing emissions by enclosure or other means. Where enclosures are used, they should be big enough and robust enough to cope with the processes, and the energy of contaminant emission or release involved. For airborne contaminants, properly designed exhaust ventilation applied to the enclosure may be needed to minimise leakage into the workplace.

303 Design work methods and organisation to minimise exposure. This normally requires clearly defined and described work methods. Organise the work to minimise the number of people exposed and the duration, frequency and level of exposure. An example would be when painting or coating a large object. If containment is not feasible, then natural ventilation may, with the right precautions, be relied on to disperse vapour. This would be done best at the end of a shift, in controlled circumstances and when fewer people will be present.

304 LEV is an important option for controlling exposure. LEV systems consist of an airmover (usually a fan), an aircleaner, ductwork, and inlet hoods or terminals. Many designers and much ventilation guidance concentrates on the airmover, aircleaner and ductwork. There is a strong tendency to treat the hood design as a minor matter often left to people onsite. Yet, if the airborne contaminant is not drawn into, or contained within, the LEV hood, exposure is likely to be poorly controlled. The hood size, shape, layout and airflow requirements should all be considered. This will define the design and airflow requirements for the other elements of the system (ductwork, fans, aircleaners etc). The hood should be designed to work effectively and cope with the way the process emits airborne contaminants. So, for instance, if the source is large or emits contaminant-laden air at high velocity, a small 'captor' type hood will not be effective. Apart from considering the process to be controlled, the LEV should be designed so that it is easy to use correctly. LEV hood design should be compatible with the system of work and the operator's requirements, such as lighting and heating. LEV hoods

Principle (c). Control exposure by measures that are proportionate to the health risk

318 The more severe the potential health effect and the greater the likelihood of it occurring, the stricter the measures required to control exposure. Control measures that are adequate will take into account the nature and severity of the hazard and the magnitude, frequency and duration of exposure. They will be proportionate to the risk.

319 Consider the consequences of failure to control exposure adequately. If the health effects arising from exposure are less serious, such as simple, reversible irritation, and are not likely to cause long-term harm, it may be sufficient to reduce exposure by simple, low-cost measures such as replacing lids on vessels or cleaning work areas regularly. In such cases, it may be unnecessary to go to greater trouble and expense to reduce the risk even further. Where the health effects arising from exposure are more serious, such as cancer, asthma, allergic dermatitis, severe disease or other irreversible and disabling health effects, and there is not enough information to establish a no-effect level (remember that biological agents will not have a no-effect level), then exposure will need to be reduced to low levels. How low these levels need to be will depend on the nature of the hazard, the likelihood of harm occurring and the degree of confidence in the information on potential health effects. The control measures necessary, in this case, might be extensive, take time to develop and implement, and be relatively costly. The measures should control the risk of both long-term (chronic) and short-term (acute) health effects.

320 Where sufficient information about the health risks has not been made available, employers have a duty to find it. CHIP[5] requires suppliers to provide sufficient information to enable the employer to decide on appropriate control measures. Information on the classification of biological agents can be found in Schedule 3. In practice, suppliers, relevant trade association or specialist advisers, such as an occupational hygienist, should be able to guide employers towards the appropriate control measures for their particular circumstances. Even where there is little information on the toxic properties of the substance or material, it is possible to make decisions about control options based on the properties of similar substances or materials.

321 Some substances have exposure benchmarks, such as Workplace Exposure Limits (WELs) or other exposure standards. If these are well-founded, they can provide useful guidance in indicating how stringent control measures need to be. If people are potentially exposed to, say, 100 times the appropriate benchmark standard, then the performance of the control measures will need to be much greater than if the potential exposure was only twice the benchmark. This is the basis of the control approaches in *COSHH essentials*[20] (paragraphs 103-105) and may be useful for substances for which there are no exposure benchmarks. However, it is important to use exposure benchmarks critically. The user should know the basis of the benchmark, how well-founded it is and any residual risks at, and below, the benchmark exposure level. Well-founded means that the standard is based on a substantial amount of evidence which allows a coherent understanding of health effects, and how these relate to exposure. This, in turn, enables decisions to be made on how health protective a standard should be. The degree to which exposure should be reduced below this standard will depend on a number of factors. These include the severity of the harm being prevented, the likelihood that harm will occur and the degree of uncertainty associated with the standard.

322 Sometimes, control measures may be selected which reduce exposure more than is strictly necessary. Usually, this occurs because some controls are more convenient and acceptable. For instance, people may prefer to wear air-fed RPE rather than filtering devices, although the protection offered by the latter would be adequate, if well fitted. Such cases do not undermine the general principle that, overall, control measures should reduce exposure to a level which minimises any risk to health.

323 Control measures should be kept under review to ensure they remain effective enough in the light of new information. Knowledge and understanding of the potential health risks from substances may change. Advances in the process and control technology and work organisation may enable changes to be made to reduce exposure. Keep abreast of, and apply, industry good practice for the control of substances hazardous to health.

Principle (d). Choose the most effective and reliable control options that minimise the escape and spread of substances hazardous to health

324 Some control options are inherently more reliable and effective than others. For example, the protection afforded by personal protective equipment (PPE) is dependent upon good fit and attention to detail. In contrast a very reliable form of control is changing the process so that less of the hazardous substance is emitted or released.

325 Choose the most effective and reliable control options for the circumstances and direct these at the main sources and causes of exposure. There is much good advice on the engineering control aspects of control measures and the application of ergonomic principles (see References and further reading).

326 There is a broad hierarchy of control options available, based on inherent reliability and likely effectiveness. COSHH regulation 7 refers to many of these options. They include:

(a)   elimination of the hazardous substance;

(b)   modification of the substance, process and/or workplace;

(c)   applying controls to the process, such as enclosures and LEV;

(d)   ways of working which minimise exposure; and

(e)   equipment or devices worn by exposed individuals.

327 The key message is that there is a hierarchy of reliability of control options and this is often linked to their effectiveness.

328 Eliminating the substance means there cannot be any exposure. Always consider elimination first. If this is not possible, a reliable form of control is to change the process so that it releases less substance. Controls applied to the process might be as effective, but will require maintenance and are unlikely to be as reliable.

329 For example, the effectiveness of an LEV hood, used to contain and remove contaminant-laden air, requires that:

(a)   the system supplying the suction to the hood is maintained regularly; and

Schedule 6

Medical surveillance

Regulation 11(2)(a) and (5)

Column 1 *Substances for which medical surveillance is appropriate*	Column 2 *Process*
Vinyl chloride monomer (VCM).	*In manufacture, production, reclamation, storage, discharge, transport, use or polymerisation.*
Nitro or amino derivatives of phenol and of benzene or its homologues.	*In the manufacture of nitro or amino derivatives of phenol and of benzene or its homologues and the making of explosives with the use of any of these substances.*
Potassium or sodium chromate or dichromate.	*In manufacture.*
Ortho-tolidine and its salts. Dianisidine and its salts. Dichlorobenzidine and its salts.	*In manufacture, formation or use of these substances.*
Auramine. Magenta.	*In manufacture.*
Carbon disulphide. Disulphur dichloride. Benzene, including benzol. Carbon tetrachloride. Trichloroethylene.	*Processes in which these substances are used, or given off as vapour, in the manufacture of indiarubber or of articles or goods made wholly or partially of indiarubber.*
Pitch.	*In manufacture of blocks of fuel consisting of coal, coal dust, coke or slurry with pitch as a binding substance.*

Schedule 7

Legislation concerned with the labelling of containers and pipes

Regulation 12(5)

The Health and Safety (Safety Signs and Signals) Regulations 1996 (SI 1996/341);

The Good Laboratory Practice Regulations 1999 (SI 1999/3106);

The Radioactive Material (Road Transport) Regulations 2002 (SI 2002/1093);

The Chemicals (Hazard Information and Packaging for Supply) Regulations 2002 (SI 2002/1689); and

The Carriage of Dangerous Goods and Use of Transportable Pressure Equipment Regulations 2004 (SI 2004/568).

Schedule 8 — Fumigations excepted from regulation 14

Regulation 14(1)

Column 1 Fumigant	Column 2 Nature of fumigation
Hydrogen cyanide.	Fumigation carried out for research. Fumigations in fumigation chambers. Fumigations in the open air to control or kill mammal pests.
Methyl bromide.	Fumigations carried out for research. Fumigations in fumigation chambers. Fumigations of soil outdoors under gas-proof sheeting where not more than 1000 kg is used in any period of 24 hours on the premises. Fumigations of soil under gas-proof sheeting in glasshouses where not more than 500 kg is used in any period of 24 hours on the premises. Fumigations of compost outdoors under gas-proof sheeting where not more than 10 kg of methyl bromide is used in any period of 24 hours on the premises. Fumigations under gas-proof sheeting inside structures other than glasshouses and mushroom houses where not more than 5 kg of methyl bromide is used in each structure during any period of 24 hours. Fumigations of soil or compost in mushroom houses where not more than 5 kg of methyl bromide is used in any one fumigation in any period of 24 hours. Fumigations of containers where not more than 5 kg of methyl bromide is used in any one fumigation in a period of 24 hours.
Phosphine.	Fumigations carried out for research. Fumigations in fumigation chambers. Fumigations under gas-proof sheeting inside structures where not more than 1 kg of phosphine in each structure is used in any period of 24 hours. Fumigation in containers where not more than 0.5 kg of phosphine is used in any one fumigation in any period of 24 hours. Fumigations in individual impermeable packages. Fumigations in the open air to control or kill mammal pests.

Schedule 9

Notification of certain fumigations

Regulation 14(2)

Part I Persons to whom notifications must be made

1   *In the case of a fumigation to be carried out within the area of a harbour authority, advance notification of fumigation shall, for the purposes of regulation 14(2)(a), be given to –*

(a)   *that authority;*

(b)   *an inspector appointed under section 19 of the 1974 Act, if that inspector so requires; and*

(c)   *where the fumigation –*

   (i)   *is to be carried out on a sea-going ship, the chief fire officer of the area in which the ship is situated and the officer in charge of the office of Her Majesty's Customs and Excise at the harbour, or*

   (ii)   *is the space fumigation of a building, the chief fire officer of the area in which the building is situated.*

2   *In the case of a fumigation, other than a fumigation to which paragraph (1) applies, advance notification of fumigation shall be given to –*

(a)   *the police officer for the time being in charge of the police station for the police district in which the fumigation is carried out;*

(b)   *an inspector appointed under section 19 of the 1974 Act, if that inspector so requires; and*

(c)   *where the fumigation is to be carried out on a sea-going ship or is the space fumigation of a building, the chief fire officer of the area in which the ship or building is situated.*

Part II Information to be given in advance notice of fumigations

3   *The information to be given in a notification made for the purposes of regulation 14(2) shall include the following –*

(a)   *the name, address and place of business of the fumigator and his telephone number;*

(b)   *the name of the person requiring the fumigation to be carried out;*

(c)   *the address and description of the premises where the fumigation is to be carried out;*

(d)   *the date on which the fumigation is to be carried out and the estimated time of commencement and completion;*

(e)   *the name of the operator in charge of the fumigation; and*

(f)   *the fumigant to be used.*

Appendix 1

Control of carcinogenic and mutagenic substances

Scope of Appendix 1

1   This Appendix applies where people are exposed, or are liable to be exposed, to substances which are defined as carcinogens or mutagens in COSHH. It gives supplementary practical guidance on those Regulations in relation to work involving exposure to these substances. It should not be read in isolation from the COSHH ACOP; both the ACOP and this Appendix are concerned with the correct matching of the precautions to the risk, and should therefore be treated as complementary.

2   While the application of this Appendix depends on the potential of a substance to cause cancer or heritable genetic damage, whether it does so in practice will depend on the type and level of exposure to it. The precautions which COSHH requires will be determined by the extent of the risk of cancers or heritable genetic damage occurring and the scope for minimising that risk.

Interpretation (regulation 2)

3   COSHH defines a carcinogen as a substance or preparation (ie a mixture or solution of two or more substances) which either:

(a)   is classified for labelling purposes as carcinogenic category 1 or 2 carrying the risk phrases R45 'May cause cancer', or R49 'May cause cancer by inhalation'; or

(b)   would be so classified if the European system for classifying substances and preparations dangerous for supply was applied (even if the law does not require this, as with certain pharmaceutical products or by-products such as hardwood dust).

Substances or processes listed in Schedule 1 to the Regulations are also included in the definition, because of historic evidence of a risk of cancer in humans, though the precise agent may be unclear.

4   Similarly, COSHH defines a mutagen as a substance or preparation which either:

(a)   is classified for labelling purposes as mutagenic category 1 or 2 carrying the risk phrase R46 'May cause heritable genetic damage'; or

(b)   would be so classified if the European system for classifying substances and preparations dangerous for supply was applied (even if the law does not require this).

5   The descriptors assigned to the three categories of carcinogens are:

Carcinogenic Category 1 – substances known to cause cancer on the basis of human experience;

Carcinogenic Category 2 – substances which it is assumed can cause cancer on the basis of reliable animal evidence;

Carcinogenic Category 3 – substances where there is only evidence in animals which is of doubtful relevance to human health (ie the evidence is not good enough for Category 1 or 2).

In the case of mutagens, there are three similar categories with analogous descriptors, based on the strength of evidence for heritable genetic damage.

6   Category 3 carcinogens, with the risk phrase R40 'Limited evidence of a carcinogenic effect', and Category 3 mutagens, with the risk phrase R68 'Possible risk of irreversible effects', are *not* included in the COSHH definitions of 'carcinogen' and 'mutagen' respectively, but are subject to the general requirements of COSHH. A comprehensive list of substances defined as carcinogens or mutagens for the purposes of COSHH is in HSE's publication *EH40/2005 Workplace exposure limits*.[27]

Prohibitions relating to certain substances (regulation 4)

7   The prohibited substances are listed in full in Schedule 2 to the Regulations. The prohibitions relating to carcinogens are:

(a)   the manufacture and use, including any process resulting in the formation of: 2-naphthylamine, benzidine, 4-aminodiphenyl, 4-nitrodiphenyl, their salts and any substance containing any of these compounds in a total concentration equal to or greater than 0.1 per cent by mass;

(b)   the import of the four substances at (a);

(c)   the use of benzene for all purposes, except in industrial processes and for the purposes of research, development and analysis. The prohibition extends to use of any other substance containing benzene in a concentration equal to or greater than 0.1 per cent by mass, except for motor fuels (covered by EC Directive 85/210/EEC) and waste (covered by EC Directive 75/442/EEC as amended by 91/156/EEC and 91/689/EEC).

8   The Health and Safety Executive may grant exemption certificates under certain conditions (see regulation 16).

Assessment of the risk to health created by work involving substances hazardous to health (regulation 6)

The importance of the assessment

9   The COSHH ACOP gives guidance on carrying out the assessment. The development of the clinical effects of cancer may take place many years after first exposure. So, there may not be any early warnings of adverse effects. Therefore, risk assessment has an especially vital role to play.

10   The employer's risk assessment should therefore:

(a)   identify whether any carcinogenic or mutagenic substances covered by COSHH are present in the workplace; if so

(b)   identify the likely level of exposure and the extent of the risk; and

(c)   use the information obtained to plan effective control measures and other precautions.

11   Annex 1 gives some further relevant information.

What the risk assessment should cover

12   The assessment for exposure to any carcinogenic or mutagenic substance should at least include details of:

(a)   whether the work can be done in some other way so that it is not necessary to use a substance hazardous to health, or whether substitution by a non-hazardous or less hazardous substance is reasonably practicable;

(b)   the type of hazard (gas, fume, dust etc);

(c)   the type and level of exposure;

(d)   the identification of any workers who may be at particular risk;

(e)   the control measures to be used to prevent or reduce exposure, and evidence that the employer has considered not employing workers at particular risk in areas where they may be exposed to carcinogenic or mutagenic substances, eg pregnant women working with a transplacental carcinogen;

(f)   operating and maintenance instructions and procedures, where relevant, to ensure that exposure is reduced to as low as is reasonably practicable;

(g)   precautions when conditions are not routine, eg maintenance activities and emergencies;

(h)   use of personal protective equipment;

(i)   monitoring procedures;

(j)   health surveillance procedures;

(k)   arrangements for consulting employees and their representatives, including procedures for reporting defects in plant or precautions, and details of essential information and training requirements.

Recording the assessment

13   Where employees are likely to be exposed to carcinogens or mutagens, it is particularly important to ensure accuracy and continuity of knowledge and action. Employers who employ five or more employees must record the significant findings of the assessment where employees are liable to be exposed to a carcinogen or mutagen, even where they assess the risk to the health of their employees as small.

Prevention or control of exposure (regulation 7)

Prevention of exposure

14   The employer's first objective must be to prevent exposure to carcinogens or mutagens. Carcinogenic or mutagenic substances should not be used or processes carried on if the employer can substitute and use a suitable non-hazardous or less hazardous substitute. However, employers should take into account the carcinogenic, mutagenic, toxic and other properties of possible chemical substitutes when considering changes.

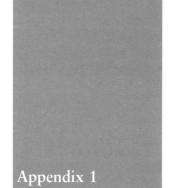

ACOP

Appendix 1

Guidance

Appendix 1

ACOP

Appendix 1

Guidance

Appendix 1

employees' exposure, so that the results can be compared with approved workplace exposure limits. If there is no approved limit for a particular carcinogenic or mutagenic substance, it is important that the employer sets an in-house occupational exposure limit to detect any deterioration in standards of control (see paragraph 129 of the ACOP).

Health surveillance (regulation 11)

23   Employers need to be aware of the objectives of health surveillance and its limitations in the case of carcinogenic or mutagenic substances.

24   Health surveillance has its limitations in identifying people at risk or in detecting signs of cancer early enough for treatment to aid a full recovery. For this reason, it is largely restricted to keeping health records, though skin cancer is a good example where appropriate health surveillance can detect the condition at an early stage when it can be cured. Medical surveillance by a medical inspector of HSE's Employment Medical Advisory Service or appointed doctor is, however, required for employees exposed to any of the substances and who are working in the related processes listed in Schedule 6. Some of the substances listed are carcinogens.

25   Health surveillance is appropriate where employees are exposed to carcinogenic or mutagenic substances, unless the employer assesses that exposure is so adequately controlled that there is no reasonable likelihood of an identifiable disease or adverse health effect resulting from the exposure (see paragraphs 222-223 of the ACOP).

26   Where there is evidence from safety data sheets, risk phrases on labels etc that a substance is known to cause, or is suspected of causing, cancer of the skin, eg arsenic, coal soot, coal tar, non-solvent refined mineral oils, contaminated used mineral oils, health surveillance should include:

(a)   regular skin inspection by a suitably qualified person; or

(b)   regular enquiries by a responsible person about any symptoms, following self-inspection by the employees concerned.

27   In other circumstances where paragraphs 25 and 26 do not apply, employers need only keep a health record, as described in paragraph 235(a) of the ACOP.

28   There is usually a long time delay between exposure to a carcinogenic substance and any related health effect. Therefore, employers should provide employees who have been exposed with information about any need for continuing health surveillance after exposure has ended, eg where a substance may cause cancer of the urinary tract.

Information, instruction and training for persons who may be exposed to substances hazardous to health (regulation 12)

29   The risk of cancer from exposure to a hazardous substance cannot in most cases be presumed to be reduced to zero except by eliminating exposure. Furthermore, the adverse effects may not show in the short term. It is, therefore, especially important that employers ensure the information, instruction and training which they provide is of an appropriately high standard. Employers should ensure that employees are aware not only of the need to maintain control of exposure, but also the additional compounding risks due to smoking. Smokers

appear to face an increased risk of occupational cancer, since they take a mixture of substances into their lungs with the smoke.

30 In addition to the information specified by COSHH and the ACOP, employers should keep employees and their safety representatives, and any other people likely to be exposed to carcinogenic or mutagenic substances, aware of:

(a)   the type or form of the risk;

(b)   the special features of carcinogenic and mutagenic substances; and

(c)   the circumstances in which they may be exposed to carcinogenic or mutagenic substances.

Annex 1 Background note on occupational cancer

1   Cancer is a disorder of cells in the body. It begins in a group of cells which fail to respond to the normal control mechanisms and continue to divide without need. The new growths which result are called tumours or neoplasia and may either be 'benign' or 'malignant'. A benign tumour is one which has remained localised, although it may produce adverse effects such as pressure on adjacent tissues and inhibition of their normal functions. Malignant tumours can invade and destroy neighbouring tissues, enter blood vessels, lymphatic vessels and other spaces, and can also be carried to tissues and organs elsewhere in the body to form new tumours, called 'secondaries' or 'metastases'. It is to these invasive, metastasising, malignant types of tumour that the term 'cancer' is generally applied.

2   Cancer may arise from various causes, one of which is the adverse effects of certain substances on cells in the body. The active agents can be the substances to which the body is exposed directly, or ones formed during the metabolism of those substances in the body. Certain substances do not cause cancer directly, but may promote or initiate it on exposure to additional substances or agents. Cancer does not necessarily arise in the sites of the body where exposure first occurs.

3   Such methods as exist for the assessment of the carcinogenicity of individual substances seldom give unequivocal results. Much research in recent years has, however, been directed at occupational cancer and there is now a growing number of substances to which varying degrees of suspicion are attached.

4   It may be very difficult to prove a causal link between a particular chemical and cancer in humans (although it can be very easy, as, for example, in the cases of vinyl chloride and angiosarcoma of the liver and bischloromethyl ether and cancer of the lung). The epidemiological data which would allow such a link to be established are often limited, if available at all. One major problem is simply that of collecting data on sufficient numbers of exposed individuals or cases: another is the delay between exposure and effect. In assessing the potential of a chemical substance to cause cancer in humans it is necessary to consider its chemical structure and its relationship to other known carcinogens, its metabolism and the results of laboratory and animal experiments. It is impossible to be more precise given the current state of knowledge.

5   The overall proportion of cancer which might be related to occupational exposure to substances hazardous to health is not known. A review[44] has suggested that approximately 4% of cancer deaths each year may be attributable to occupational hazards and a substantial number of these could be reduced if exposure to the risks was adequately controlled. In Great Britain on average each year from 1996 to 2000, there were approximately 78 000 cancer deaths among men and approximately 72 000 among women aged 15 and over. This equals in total to approximately 6000 occupation-related cancer deaths per year in males and females aged 15 and over. It may be difficult to identify causative agents, or to assess with accuracy the degree of risk involved at any given exposure, because:

(a)   there is often a long period between exposure and effect;

(b)   some types of malignant disease such as lung cancer are relatively common in the population at large, and therefore an excess incidence among people exposed to particular substances may pass undetected;

(c)   histories of occupational exposure are seldom recorded;

(d) other factors such as smoking, diet, lifestyle or exposure to other substances or agents may act separately or synergistically with occupational factors to affect the incidence of cancer;

(e) some carcinogenic agents such as environmental tobacco smoke are present in both work and non-work situations; and

(f) the cause of death may not be accurately recorded on death certificates, and the changing pattern of cancer survival makes sole reliance on death certificates an inadequate indicator of true cancer incidence.

6   Even for substances identified as having the ability to cause cancer in humans, the degree of risk involved in handling them varies depending on factors such as their potency, the physical form or concentration in which they are present, the manner of use and the precautions which are applied to minimise exposure. As with any type of hazardous substance the overall objective is to ensure that the risk is eliminated or reduced to extremely low levels by the adoption of control measures and other precautions which are appropriate to the nature and degree of risk in each case. The principles of occupational health, including those of occupational medicine and hygiene and the practical means by which exposure to substances hazardous to health is assessed, monitored and controlled, are no different for carcinogenic substances than for those involving other health hazards. The COSHH (Amendment) Regulations 1992 (now revoked and replaced by COSHH 2002) introduced special provisions for prevention or control of exposure to carcinogens. But it should also be noted that many substances which are known to be carcinogenic are also likely to present additional hazards, such as acute toxicity, which also need to be controlled. Measures adequate to control toxicity, however, may not necessarily provide adequate control against cancer.

7   There are a number of important reasons which, taken together, require special attention to be given to the control of exposure to carcinogenic substances:

(a) most forms of cancer carry a high risk of premature death. Although new forms of surveillance and treatment have improved the prognosis in some cases. Prevention is better than cure for all diseases, but, in the case of occupational cancer, preventing or reducing the incidence of the condition by eliminating or minimising exposure to the causative agents may be the only effective remedy;

(b) the mechanisms by which carcinogenic substances exert their effects are not fully understood and, in most cases, there are no established scientific methods by which to determine what if any, thresholds exist below which individuals are at no risk from exposure. So, in the present state of knowledge, it is usually not possible to specify any wholly 'safe' limits;

(c) there is commonly a long delay, sometimes decades, between first exposure and the occurrence of cancer. As a consequence of this 'latent period' there is no short-term indication that a particular person exposed to carcinogenic substances is being adversely affected;

(d) cancer is more feared than most other causes of death, because of the association with pain and the uncertainty of the period between diagnosis and the outcome of treatment.

8   This Appendix deals with those specific substances and processes defined in regulation 2 of COSHH with which a cancer hazard is associated. This does not imply that all other substances or processes present no cancer hazard or that appropriate precautions are not necessary where this Appendix does not apply. Medical research continues to discover further substances and processes to which varying degrees of suspicion of causing cancer are attached. These include substances classified as a carcinogen Category 3; R40 ('Limited evidence of a carcinogenic effect') under CHIP. For these substances and processes, HSE recommends a precautionary policy of prevention and control based on up-to-date knowledge of the substance suspected of being carcinogenic but not defined as a carcinogen under COSHH. This policy is set out in paragraphs 24-25 of the COSHH ACOP.

9   This background note addresses occupational cancer, but these are not the only hazards of cancer that are likely to be encountered during the working day. They constitute only a small proportion of the total risk of cancer (see Table 3). Industry can help to reduce the total risk by ensuring that workers have an opportunity to work not only where the risks from defined specific industrial carcinogens are prevented or adequately controlled, but where they can also work in an atmosphere:

(a)   free from tobacco smoke (smoking is responsible for some 33% of all deaths from cancer and about 25% of all cases of lung cancer in non-smokers are attributable to environmental tobacco smoke (Wald et al, 1986).[45] The 1998 SCOTH report[46] said that smoking is the predominant cause of lung cancer with approximately 90% of lung cancer deaths in Western populations attributable to cigarette usage. Passive smoking in non-smokers over a substantial part of their life is associated with a 10-30% increase in the risk of lung cancer, which could account for several hundred lung cancers a year in the UK;

(b)   free from high concentrations of natural radon (radon is estimated to cause about 6% of all lung cancers, mostly in synergism with smoking);[47]

(c)   where they have an opportunity when they take meals at work, of eating foods that will help to reduce rather than increase the risk of cancer.[48]

Table 3 Proportion of cancer deaths attributable to different factors (modified from Doll and Peto, 1981)

Factor	Per cent of cancer deaths	
	Certain	Possible*
Tobacco	33	35
Diet	10	60
Natural radiation (sunlight, radon etc)	4	4
Alcohol	3	4
Natural hormones	2	20
Occupation	2	6
Viruses	2	5
Pollution and industrial products	< 1	5
Medicines and medical procedures	< 1	1
Other and unknown	0	?

* The percentages of 'possibles' add up to more than 100% because the influences of some 'causes' may be combined with other causes (eg radon and smoking).

Failure of plant giving rise to increased concentrations

9   Employers should identify, investigate and remedy immediately any failure or malfunction of a part of the plant or apparatus or any other occurrence that gives rise to, or is liable to give rise to, unusually large increases in the concentration of vinyl chloride in the working environment.

Maintenance

10   Employers should maintain all plant to a high standard, especially that from which vinyl chloride may escape, to limit the exposure of workers to vinyl chloride.

Automatic monitoring systems

11   Employers must ensure that adequate control is maintained in the event of any foreseen increases in the concentration of vinyl chloride in the workplace. To do this they should use an automatic monitoring system which is capable of detecting such increases in places where they may reasonably be expected to occur. Employers should take similar precautions during plant maintenance.

Alarm levels

12   The following concentrations of vinyl chloride in the atmosphere of a working area should be treated as alarm levels signalling the need for remedial action:

(a)   15 ppm when measured over a period of 1 hour; or

(b)   20 ppm when measured over a period of 20 minutes; or

(c)   30 ppm when measured over a period of 2 minutes.

13   Any person who remains in the area while the alarm lasts should wear suitable RPE that will provide adequate control of exposure.

Suitable respiratory protective equipment

14   Any respiratory protective equipment (RPE) the employer provides must be capable of adequately controlling the employees' exposure to vinyl chloride. To be suitable, it must be correctly selected and used, and correctly matched to the job and to the employee who will wear it (see paragraphs 148-153 of the main ACOP). For vinyl chloride the most appropriate RPE is compressed-air line or self-contained breathing apparatus complying with the Personal Protective Equipment Regulations 2002.

When respiratory protective equipment must be worn

15   RPE must be worn:

(a)   by any person remaining in a working area where exposure is liable to exceed the 8-hour TWA WEL, eg to check for and stop a leakage, following an alarm as a result of abnormal increases in the concentration of airborne vinyl chloride;

(b)   when opening equipment which may release large quantities of vinyl chloride to the atmosphere, eg during the maintenance or repair of equipment and when it is not reasonably practicable to remove the vapour by local exhaust ventilation. This release operation should not be carried out without a 'permit-to-work' issued by a responsible person appointed by the employer. A permit-to-work is essentially a document which sets out the work to be done and the precautions to be taken. It predetermines a safe procedure and is a clear record that all foreseeable hazards have been considered in advance and that all appropriate precautions are defined and taken in correct sequence. It does not, in itself, make the job safe but is dependent for its effectiveness on those concerned conscientiously carrying out the requirements of the permit. Employers should also take precautions to ensure that other unprotected personnel in the vicinity are not liable to be exposed to concentrations of vinyl chloride above the 8-hour TWA WEL following its release;

(c)   during entry into confined spaces where concentrations of vinyl chloride in air are liable to be above the 8-hour TWA WEL.

Personal protective equipment

16   Under normal circumstances, where vinyl chloride is reliably contained within enclosed plant, there may be no need for employees to wear special protective clothing. However, certain circumstances, such as entry into confined spaces or some maintenance work, may require the use of suitable protective clothing, eg to prevent absorption of the substance through the skin. These situations should be identified as part of the risk assessment. The standard of clothing necessary will depend on the form exposure takes and how long it lasts.

Monitoring exposure in the workplace (regulation 10)

17   Regulation 10, together with Schedule 5, require employers to monitor the concentrations of airborne vinyl chloride in working areas to estimate the exposure of employees, including any maintenance workers, and to monitor the effectiveness of all control measures.

Objectives

18   The objectives of monitoring are:

(a)   to verify that any technical measures provided are controlling employees' exposure to vinyl chloride as far as is reasonably practicable to below the WEL;

(b)   to detect any abnormal increases in vinyl chloride-in-air levels occurring as a result of the failure or malfunction of some part of the plant or apparatus by using the short-term alarm levels; and

(c)   to complement health surveillance procedures towards the detection and evaluation of risks to health.

Suitable procedures for monitoring

19   In order to be effective, arrangements for monitoring require careful planning. Employers should draw up a formal air monitoring plan and bring it to the attention of all employees working in areas where vinyl chloride is liable to be present. The plan should contain details of air monitoring procedures and equipment, including:

(a) the parts of plant, working areas and occupational groups of employees to be monitored;

(b) the type of air sampling to be carried out in each of the areas concerned, ie personal air sampling and/or fixed point air sampling;

(c) the frequency of air sampling and the siting of air sampling equipment so that the results obtained accurately reflect the conditions to which employees are likely to be exposed;

(d) the types of sampling and analytical equipment to be used;

(e) the arrangements for the testing and calibration of sampling and analytical equipment;

(f) the statistical analysis and presentation of the air sampling results.

20 Employers should use information from the initial and any subsequent assessments when planning or revising the details of the monitoring procedures.

Sampling methods

21 The main method used routinely for ensuring that exposure is below the WEL and alarm levels will be static sampling. To assess compliance in respect of the 8-hour TWA WEL, personal monitoring is necessary. Measuring instruments should always be calibrated regularly, in accordance with the manufacturers' current instructions.

22 Schedule 5 to COSHH requires that continuous or permanent sequential (which is equivalent to continuous) methods of static sampling must be used. Alternatively, except for enclosed vinyl chloride polymerisation plants, discontinuous methods may be used instead.

Monitoring when vinyl chloride is handled intermittently

23 Where vinyl chloride is handled intermittently, monitoring of exposures by personal sampling should be carried out sufficiently often to ensure that the technical control measures and working procedures adopted as adequate to keep exposure below the WEL.

24 If a non-selective method of sampling and measurement is used, ie it cannot distinguish between vinyl chloride monomer and any other substance that may have been caught by the sampler, the measurement recorded should be regarded as the concentration of vinyl chloride monomer in the air.

Measuring points

25 Employers should choose measuring points which produce results that are as representative as possible of employees' exposure to vinyl chloride in the area. Large working areas will normally require more than one monitoring point and in these situations the average value of all the measurements recorded should be used to compare it with the WEL to determine whether adequate control is being maintained.

Records

26   Employers should include the following information in the monitoring records:

(a)   For excursions above the alarm levels detected during area monitoring:

    (i)   the part of factory to which the record refers;

    (ii)   the precise location within the factory;

    (iii)   the date, time and (where known) duration;

    (iv)   the maximum and time-weighted average concentrations recorded;

    (v)   the results of investigation;

    (vi)   the action taken;

    (vii)   the name, signature and appointment of the person making the investigation;

(b)   personal monitoring: the name of the employee, date, time and duration of exposure, time-weighted average concentrations recorded and precise locations within the factory. These should be summarised on a monthly basis, by job category in each plant, in addition to shift results.

27   In the areas where continuous sampling equipment is installed, employers should ensure that results are summarised for each shift and for each identifiable working area showing the average air concentration in that area. Each new series of records should include details of the position and number of sampling points, and the frequency of sampling and analytical methods used. Afterwards, this information need only be recorded when changes are made to the monitoring procedure.

28   In those working areas where sampling is not carried out on each shift, the time-weighted average results should be recorded and summarised on a monthly basis showing the average concentration at each location, with an analysis of the distribution of the results.

Health surveillance (regulation 11)

Suitable health surveillance

29   COSHH regulation 11 and Schedule 6 require employers to place all employees exposed to vinyl chloride under health surveillance, unless there is no reasonable likelihood that an identifiable disease or adverse health effect will result from their exposure.

30   Where health surveillance is appropriate, it must include:

(a)   the keeping of a health record for every employee concerned, containing the details set out in paragraph 235 of the COSHH ACOP;

(b)   medical surveillance under the supervision of a medical inspector of HSE's Employment Medical Advisory Service or appointed doctor before starting work, and at intervals of not more than 12 months, or at such shorter intervals, as the medical inspector or doctor may require; and

(c) a review of the health records.

31 The medical surveillance of each individual is the responsibility of the doctor concerned but should normally include:

(a) a full medical and occupational history;

(b) a clinical assessment with particular reference to the abdomen, skin and extremities; and

(c) such further tests, including radiological examination and laboratory tests, as may be indicated by the results of (a) or (b).

Information, instruction and training (regulation 12)

Information

32 The information which employees should be given who work with or are liable to be exposed to VCM is set out in regulation 12 and its supporting guidance. Wherever practicable, this information should be given when the employee attends for the initial medical examination.

Appendix 2

Additional provisions relating to work with biological agents

Scope of Appendix 2

1   This Appendix, which includes ACOP and guidance, applies only to deliberate work (ie work involving research, development, teaching or diagnostics) with biological agents (see paragraphs 48-49 of the main ACOP text for types of exposure), as defined in COSHH.

2   It should be read in conjunction with the main ACOP and guidance. The main ACOP gives practical guidance on those aspects of COSHH which are common to all work where there may be incidental exposure to biological agents (eg risk assessment, preventive/control methods and emergency measures).

Classification of biological agents (Schedule 3, paragraph 2)

3   Any biological agent which appears in the classification list approved by the Health and Safety Commission (referred to as the Approved List of biological agents)13 is categorised as being in the hazard group (HG) specified there.

4   The definition of 'biological agent' includes:

(a)   micro-organisms such as bacteria, viruses, fungi;

(b)   the agents that cause transmissible spongiform encephalopathies (TSEs);

(c)   parasites (eg, malarial parasites, amoebae and trypanosomes);

(d)   the microscopic infectious forms of larger parasites (eg the ova and infectious larval forms of helminths); and

(e)   cell cultures and human endoparasites, providing they have one or more of the harmful properties in the definition (cause any infection, allergy, toxicity or otherwise create a hazard to human health).

Nucleic acid is not a biological agent, however, it can still be a substance hazardous to health, eg oncogenic DNA sequences are able to make cells tumorigenic. In such cases the more general provisions outlined in COSHH would apply.

5   Biological agents are classified into four hazard groups according to their ability to cause infection in healthy humans, the severity of the disease that may result, the risk that infection will spread to the community, and the availability of vaccines and effective treatment. (This does not remove the duty to consider appropriate aspects of an individual's health when performing a biological agent risk assessment under COSHH, the Management Regulations[17] or other legislation.) Some biological agents are not infectious at all but the infection criteria are the only ones used for classification purposes, even though a biological agent may have toxic, allergenic or other harmful properties. While a non-infectious biological agent may be classified as a Hazard Group 1 agent, substantial control measures may still be needed for it, depending on the other harmful properties it has. For example if it has toxic properties, then COSHH would apply.

6   Biological agents may also be classified as genetically modified micro-organisms (GMMs), but not all GMMs are biological agents. While COSHH

covers the risks to human health, additional controls (see paragraph 19 of this Appendix) may be required under the Genetically Modified Organisms (Contained Use) Regulations 2000 (as amended)[51] to control risks to the environment. Zoonotic biological agents (disease of animals that can be transmitted to humans) may also be controlled under Department for the Environment, Food and Rural Affairs (DEFRA) animal health legislation (eg Specified Animal Pathogens Order 1988[52] and Importation of Animal Pathogens Order 1980).[53]

7　The Approved List of biological agents is not exhaustive and a biological agent that does not appear on the list should not automatically be classified as Hazard Group 1 agent. The appropriate group for an unclassified agent should be determined by the employer by applying the infection criteria in Schedule 3, paragraph 2 and taking into account the relevant factors used in making the risk assessment required by Regulation 6 of COSHH. If the agent subsequently appears in a later edition of the Approved List, the classification given to it in that edition takes priority.

8　**Where an employer is using a biological agent which has an approved classification, but where the risk of infection for that particular agent is different to that expected from the approved classification, the employer shall reclassify the agent as if performing a provisional classification under Schedule 3, paragraph 2, sub-paragraph (2). Employers should consult and agree with HSE that a suitable and sufficient risk assessment has been performed prior to locally reclassifying an agent, unless specific HSE guidance indicating what to do in specific circumstances has been published.**

9　With certain agents or strains of agents which have an approved classification, the risk of infection may be greater or less than expected. Examples include subspecies, naturally occurring mutants, some genetically modified agents and attenuated vaccine strains. Such agents may be treated as though they were different from the named agent that appears on the Approved List and reclassified as if performing a provisional classification. Suitable control and containment can then be selected accordingly. Employers should also take into account the type of work to be carried out, the quantity of material to be handled and the degree of exposure when determining the most appropriate control and containment measures for such agents.

10　Agents which have been modified in such a way that they are more hazardous than the named agent which appears in the Approved List should be regarded as though they were classified in a higher hazard group.

Special control measures for laboratories, animal rooms and industrial processes (Schedule 3, paragraph 3)

11　**For laboratories, animal rooms and industrial processes, the appropriate containment level is derived from the hazard classification of the agent, or from what is suspected about the possible presence of an agent. COSHH requires that when working with an agent (eg propagation or concentration) in a particular hazard group, the containment level selected must match the hazard group of the agent as a minimum.**

12　Special measures are required in laboratories, animal rooms and industrial processes that involve the use of biological agents, to ensure that the agents are not transmitted to workers or released outside the containment facility. Where work is being carried out which increases the risk of exposure to an agent in a particular hazard group (eg concentration, or working with large volumes of the agent), this requires all the containment measures from the matching containment level to be used. So, work with a Hazard Group 2 agent must be carried out at Containment Level 2 etc (but see paragraphs 15-17 of this Appendix).

13 Laboratories that work with potentially infectious material, but where it is unlikely that Group 3 or 4 agents are present, should achieve Containment Level 2 as a minimum (Schedule 3, paragraph 3(4)(d)). For example, laboratories performing routine diagnostic work (eg processing of specimens in biochemistry or haematology laboratories) should be generally working at Level 2.

14 Schedule 3, paragraph 3(4)(e) requires that laboratories that do not intentionally propagate or concentrate biological agents, but where the presence of agents calling for Containment Levels 3 or 4 is nevertheless known or likely, based on the information provided with the specimen, should use the appropriate containment levels (but see paragraph 15 below). For example, a water company laboratory carrying out routine screening of water supplies would normally work at Containment Level 2. However, if there is information that supplies are being externally contaminated then Level 3 may be required, depending on the source of contamination.

15 There are certain circumstances where not all the containment measures at a particular level may be necessary, either because of the nature of the agent being handled or the type of work being undertaken. However, at present, this applies only to certain Hazard Group 3 (HG3) agents specified on the Approved List of Biological Agents www.hse.gov.uk/pubns/misc208.pdf.[13] HSC has produced accepted procedures for reducing the containment measures for these HG3 agents.

16 There may be other circumstances or types of work involving agents from other hazard groups where HSC considers the full containment measures may not be appropriate. Guidance may be issued on these. This Appendix and guidance sets out the general approach. But, in many cases, more specific advice on suitable containment and control measures is available in guidance issued by the HSC, eg *Transmissible spongiform encephalopathy agents: Safe working and the prevention of infection*. (A list of relevant HSC guidance publications can be found at www.hse.gov.uk/biosafety/information.htm). Such guidance may indicate that although certain measures may be dispensed with, other additional precautions or procedures may be required to ensure safe working. Employers should be sure of the scope and meaning of guidance before making a decision to dispense with certain measures on the basis of it, and if in doubt should consult HSE.

17 Examples of likely situations where full Containment Level 3 may not be required are:

(a) work where, although there is a strong indication or likelihood that certain Hazard Group 3 agents might be present, the work will not lead to an increase in the risk of exposure to the agent. For example, blood-borne viruses (BBV) are unlikely to infect by an airborne route during diagnostic procedures not involving propagation or concentration of the virus, eg haematology, testing blood donations for transfusion, serology and drug assays. Providing appropriate precautions are taken, not all the stated Containment Level 3 measures may be required;

(b) intentional work with agents whose unique biological properties, such as the agents that cause transmissible spongiform encephalopathies (TSEs) or certain parasites, means that certain measures are not required to control the risk of exposure. For example, fumigation is ineffective against TSEs, so the laboratory would not need to be sealable for fumigation.

18 A biological agent that is classified in Hazard Group 1 under COSHH may also be classified as a GMM under the Genetically Modified Organisms

(Contained Use) Regulations 2000 (as amended). Such agents may require additional containment measures because of environmental risks associated with them. The standards described in the Contained Use Regulations are broadly equivalent to those in COSHH, but where there is a difference, the more stringent requirements should be followed.

19   As well as determining the containment level appropriate for the particular activity involving research, development, teaching or diagnostic work with a biological agent (according to Schedule 3, paragraph 3), it is important to identify and introduce any other control measures necessary to adequately control exposure to the biological agent (regulations 6 and 7 of COSHH).

List of employees exposed to certain biological agents (Schedule 3, paragraph 4)

20   Employers are required to keep a list of employees who are exposed to Hazard Group 3 or 4 biological agents during work of a research, development, teaching or diagnostic nature with the agent or, in cases of unintentional exposure, if a risk assessment shows there is a significant risk. The risk is deemed to be significant if more than basic hygiene measures are necessary to protect staff or if the control measures listed in COSHH are specifically applied. Such records can be kept in whatever format is most appropriate for the undertaking. Any health or medical surveillance records kept are subject to the requirements of the Data Protection Act 1998.[54]

21   The list required by Schedule 3, paragraph 4 is not the same as a health record kept in accordance with regulation 11. The decision to keep a list will depend on a local risk assessment. It is important to emphasise that the list is required where there is a likelihood of exposure, not simply when there has been a known incident or accident (although it should also include details of these). In this sense it is not the same as the requirement to report certain diseases and accidents to HSE under the Reporting of Injuries, Diseases and Dangerous Occurrences Regulations 1995 (RIDDOR).[55]

22   For some types of work, eg normal patient management, the risk may not be significant, and so a list may not be needed. However, where staff are performing invasive clinical procedures on patients suspected of being infected with a Group 3 or 4 agent, additional control and containment measures may be required. As this risk is significant, employees should be listed as being potentially exposed.

23   Exposure to certain biological agents may result in infections capable of establishing persistent or latent infections, long incubation periods, or may have serious long-term consequences. Record-keeping requirements have therefore been aligned with those in Regulation 11(3) of COSHH, which requires that health records be kept for 40 years.

Notification of the use of biological agents (Schedule 3, paragraph 5)

24   Schedule 3, paragraph 5 requires that certain activities involving biological agents should be notified to HSE, unless notification has already been made under the Genetically Modified Organisms (Contained Use) Regulations 2000 (as amended). Notice must be given:

(a)   of an intention to use agents from a particular hazard group, other than HG1, for the first time at a particular premises; and

(b)   of each subsequent use of a new biological agent which is specified in Part V of Schedule 3.

25 Notification is required when premises are to be used for the first time for research, development, teaching or diagnostic activities with a Hazard Group 2, 3 or 4 agent, eg propagation, concentration or storage before use. For example, when an agent is acquired, even if just for a culture collection, it is likely that there will be an intention to use it, eg for quality and control aspects of maintaining the culture collection. Employers who provide a diagnostic service for HG2 and HG3 agents which does not involve propagation of the agents are exempted from notification requirements. For example some diagnostic tests require the propagation of agents, eg rabies virus (HG3) for testing animal immunity. Such services would require notification.

26 The only exception is the provision of diagnostic services in relation to Group 4 agents. This activity must meet the requirements outlined in paragraph 24(a) whether or not there is an intention to grow the agents.

27 The extent to which groups of premises (for example, different laboratories within the same research institution, university or hospital; geographically separate parts of an institute/company etc) may be the subject of a single notification will depend largely on the way in which the management structure of the employer making the notification is organised. For example, if several laboratories within one organisation were working on an agent as part of the same project, this could be a single notification. However, different groups working on the same agent for different reasons (eg different projects), would have to submit separate notifications.

28 HSE must be notified in writing of an employer's intention at least 20 working days in advance, and an employer cannot use the biological agent until the notification has been acknowledged by HSE. This acknowledgement is not an approval of how the employer will work with the biological agent concerned.

29 A single notification could cover a programme of work which includes a combination of activities and/or combination of agents in different hazard groups. However, to form a connected programme they must all be part of a coherent and integrated programme of work. That is, they should all form part of a specific scientific/research goal. One good indicator of whether the activities are sufficiently connected is if they would be acceptable as a single, standard research grant application.

30 Notification of subsequent use of HG2, HG3 and HG4 agents as specified in Schedule 3 Part V is required when a different agent is to be used from that identified in the original notification, ie another strain, or where the risk of infection is different to that expected for the agent previously nominated. New notification forms are available from HSE, with further supporting guidance on when to notify first use, subsequent use, or consignment of biological agents.

Notification of the consignment of biological agents (Schedule 3, paragraph 6)

31 Schedule 3, paragraph 6(1) requires that prior notification is given to HSE when a Hazard Group 4 biological agent or anything known or suspected of containing such an agent is to be consigned to other premises. This requirement does not apply if the consignment is for the purpose of diagnosis or disposal, or the medical treatment of a human or animal.

32 A single set of premises may include more than one building, and transportation from one to another in such a case is not notifiable.

Assessment of the risk to health created by work involving substances hazardous to health (regulation 6)

7   The risk assessment should:

(a)   identify the hazards – which substances with the potential to cause asthma are used or generated by work activity;

(b)   decide who might be harmed, and how. Which routine and non-routine activities of employees and others are likely to involve exposure? In deciding who might be harmed, it might be prudent to consider also who might be more at risk/vulnerable;

(c)   evaluate the risks and decide whether existing precautions are adequate or if more should be done. See if exposure can be prevented and, if it cannot, consider the potential risk for each activity. Consider whether the substances identified might be released into the air as a result of the work activity;

(d)   record the findings – employers with five or more employees must record the significant findings, eg hazards and conclusions;

(e)   review the assessment and revise it if necessary. Identify all relevant measures to provide adequate control and ensure their combined effectiveness.

8   Assessment of control measures and good working practices for substances which cause asthma should take account of the seriousness of the health effects which could result from a failure of control. Particular attention should be given to identifying and assessing the controls for any short-term exposures which may involve markedly higher concentrations than the long-term average.

9   Employers are required by COSHH to protect the health of employees who have developed occupational asthma even though they may develop symptoms at very low, even undetectable, levels of exposure.

10   Employers should review assessments regularly as required by regulation 6(3) of COSHH. There should be arrangements for review of the assessment and control measures in the light of experience or if new information becomes available. It is particularly important that there should be an immediate review wherever a case of occupational asthma is confirmed.

11   The employer should set out procedures for responding to a confirmed new case of asthma, which may be occupationally related. These should include measures to:

(a)   protect the person(s) while the cause of the symptoms is investigated;

(b)   review the assessment and control measures; and

(c)   report the case to the enforcing authority if a doctor has notified the employer of it in writing. This is required by RIDDOR.

Prevention or control of exposure to substances hazardous to health (regulation 7)

12   Exposure to substances with the potential to cause occupational asthma should be prevented. If that is not reasonably practicable, the objective should be to control exposure so as to prevent employees and others who may be exposed

from developing occupational asthma as a result of exposure to those substances. Limited scientific knowledge on levels below which substances will not cause asthma means that it will be necessary to reduce exposure so far as is reasonably practicable. This will involve considering the potential for short-term peaks of exposure as well as longer-term time-weighted averages.

13 If an individual develops occupational asthma to a substance, their exposure must be controlled to prevent triggering further attacks. Suitable levels are likely to be well below any workplace exposure level, where these exist.

Health surveillance (regulation 11)

14 All employees exposed or liable to be exposed to a substance which may cause occupational asthma should be under suitable health surveillance. The extent and detail of the health surveillance should be related to the degree of risk identified during the COSHH assessment. There should be appropriate consultation with an occupational health professional over the degree of risk and level of surveillance. Health surveillance should include the maintenance of a health record in a suitable form for each exposed individual.

Information, instruction and training for persons who may be exposed to substances hazardous to health (regulation 12)

15 Employees should be provided with suitable and sufficient information covering in particular:

(a) typical symptoms of asthma;

(b) the nature of any substance likely to cause occupational asthma to which they may be exposed;

(c) the likelihood that once developed, occupational asthma could be permanent and what happens after further exposures;

(d) the procedures for reporting symptoms; and

(e) the need to report immediately any symptoms which may indicate that asthma has occurred.

16 Employers should also give employees proper training, including induction training before they start the job. Appropriate training should be given in respect of:

(a) correct use and maintenance of the control measures provided;

(b) work practices which prevent or reduce the emission of the substance into the atmosphere of both the workplace and the general environment;

(c) the use of RPE, where it is used as a control measure, and other control measures to further reduce exposure to the substance; and

(d) emergency procedures.

References and further reading

References

1   *The Control of Substances Hazardous to Health Regulations 2002* SI 2002/2677 The Stationery Office 2002 ISBN 0 11 042919 2

2   *The Control of Substances Hazardous to Health (Amendment) Regulations 2003* SI 2003/978 The Stationery Office 2003 ISBN 0 11 045572 X

3   *The Control of Substances Hazardous to Health (Amendment) Regulations 2004* SI 2004/3386 The Stationery Office 2004 ISBN 0 11 051407 6

4   *Protection of the health and safety of workers from the risks related to chemical agents at work* EC Directive (98/24/EC)

5   *Approved classification and labelling guide. Chemicals (Hazard Information and Packaging for Supply) Regulations 2002. Guidance on Regulations* L131 (Fifth edition) HSE Books 2002 ISBN 0 7176 2369 6

6   *The Coal Mines (Respirable Dust) (Amendment) Regulations 1978* The Stationery Office 1978 ISBN 0 11 083807 6

7   *Medicines Act 1968 Ch 67* The Stationery Office 1968 ISBN 0 10 546768 5

8   *Consulting employees on health and safety: A guide to the law* Leaflet INDG232 HSE Books 1996 (single copy free or priced packs of 15 ISBN 0 7176 1615 0)

9   *Approved supply list. Information approved for the classification and labelling of substances and preparations dangerous for supply. Chemicals (Hazard Information and Packaging for Supply) Regulations 2002. Approved list* L129 (Seventh edition) HSE Books 2002 ISBN 0 7176 2368 8

10   BS EN 481: 1993 *Workplace atmospheres. Size fraction definitions for measurement of airborne particles* British Standards Institution

11   *Dangerous Substances and Explosive Atmospheres. Dangerous Substances and Explosive Atmospheres Regulations 2002. Approved Code of Practice and guidance* L138 HSE Books 2003 ISBN 0 7176 2203 7

12   *Safe work in confined spaces. Confined Spaces Regulations 1997. Approved Code of Practice, Regulations and guidance* L101 HSE Books 1997 ISBN 0 7176 1405 0

13   *The Approved List of biological agents* HSE 2005 Web version only available at www.hse.gov.uk/pubns/misc208.pdf

14   *Workplace health, safety and welfare. Workplace (Health, Safety and Welfare) Regulations 1992. Approved Code of Practice* L24 HSE Books 1992 ISBN 0 7176 0413 6

15   *Consumer Protection Act 1987 Ch 43* The Stationery Office 1987 ISBN 0 10 544387 5

16   *Risk assessment reports* published by the European Union in connection with work carried out in accordance with Council Regulation (EEC) 793/93 Web versions available at http://ecb.jrc.it/existing-chemicals

17   *Management of health and safety at work. Management of Health and Safety at Work Regulations 1999. Approved Code of Practice and guidance* L21 (Second edition) HSE Books 2000 ISBN 0 7176 2488 9

18   *Health and Safety at Work etc Act 1974 Ch37* The Stationery Office 1974 ISBN 0 10 543774 3

19   *The Prescription Only Medicines (Human Use) Order 1997* SI 1997/2044 The Stationery Office 1997 ISBN 0 11 064858 7

20   *COSHH essentials: Easy steps to control chemicals. Control of Substances Hazardous to Health Regulations* HSG193 (Second edition) HSE Books 2003 ISBN 0 7176 2737 3 (a web version is available at www.coshh-essentials.org.uk)

21   *The technical basis for COSHH essentials: Easy steps to control chemicals* HSE Books 1999 ISBN 0 7176 2434 X

22   *A step by step guide to COSHH assessment* HSG97 (Second edition) HSE Books 2004 ISBN 0 7176 2785 3

23   *Seven steps to successful substitution of hazardous substances* HSG110 HSE Books 1994 ISBN 0 7176 0695 3

24   *Asthmagen? Critical assessments of the evidence for agents implicated in occupational asthma* HSE Books 1997 ISBN 0 7176 1465 4

25   *An introduction to local exhaust ventilation* HSG37 (Second edition) HSE Books 1993 ISBN 0 7176 1001 2

26   *General ventilation in the workplace: Guidance for employers* HSG202 HSE Books 2000 ISBN 0 7176 1793 9

27   *EH40/2005 Workplace exposure limits: Containing the list of workplace exposure limits for use with the Control of Substances Hazardous to Health Regulations 2002* Environmental Hygiene Guidance Note EH40 HSE Books 2005 ISBN 0 7176 2977 5

28   Web only versions of CHANs available at www.hse.gov.uk/pubns/chindex.htm

29   *Monitoring strategies for toxic substances* HSG173 HSE Books 1997 ISBN 0 7176 1411 5

30   *Health risk management: A guide to working with solvents* HSG188 HSE Books 1998 ISBN 0 7176 1664 9

31   *Biological monitoring in the workplace: A guide to its practical application to chemical exposure* HSG167 HSE Books 1997 ISBN 0 7176 1279 1

32   *Personal protective equipment at work. Personal Protective Equipment at Work Regulations 1992. Guidance on Regulations* L25 HSE Books 1992 ISBN 0 7176 0415 2

33   *Respiratory protective equipment at work: A practical guide* HSG53 (Third edition) HSE Books 2005 ISBN 0 7176 2904 X

34   *Fit testing of respiratory protective equipment facepieces* OC 282/28(rev) HSE 2003. Web only version available at www.hse.gov.uk/pubns/fittesting.pdf

35   *Accreditation for the inspection of local exhaust ventilating (LEV) plant* RG4 United Kingdom Accreditation Service (UKAS) 2000 (available from UKAS, 21-47 High St, Feltham, Middlesex TW13 4UN Tel: 020 8917 8400 (9 am-1 pm) Fax: 020 8917 8500 Website: www.ukas.com)

36   *Maintenance, examination and testing of local exhaust ventilation* HSG54 (Second edition) HSE Books 1998 ISBN 0 7176 1485 9

37   BS 4275: 1997 *Guide to implementing an effective respiratory protective device programme* British Standards Institution

38   *The Control of Pesticides Regulations 1986* SI 1986/1510 The Stationery Office 1986 ISBN 0 11 067510 X

39   *A guide to the Health and Safety (Consultation with Employees) Regulations 1996. Guidance on Regulations* L95 HSE Books 1996 ISBN 0 7176 1234 1

40   *Safety representatives and safety committees* L87 (Third edition) HSE Books 1996 ISBN 0 7176 1220 1

41   BS 1710: 1984 *Specification for identification of pipelines and services* British Standards Institution

42   *The Control of Major Accident Hazards Regulations 1999* SI 1999/743 The Stationery Office 1999 ISBN 0 11 082192 0

43   *First aid at work. The Health and Safety (First Aid) Regulations 1981. Approved Code of Practice and guidance* L74 HSE Books 1997 ISBN 0 7176 1050 0

44   Doll Sir Richard *Carcinogenic risk: Getting it in proportion* (paper in conference proceedings: Cancer in the workplace 15 October 1992, HSE and Society of Chemical Industry)

45   *Passive smoking at work* Leaflet INDG63(rev1) HSE Books 1992 (internet version only)

46   Poswillo D *Report of the Scientific Committee on Tobacco and Health* The Stationery Office 1998 ISBN 0 11 322124 X

47   *Radon in the workplace* Leaflet INDG210 HSE Books 1995 (single copy free)

48   *Nutritional aspects of the development of cancer* Health Education Authority ISBN 0 75211100 0

50   *The Special Waste Regulations 1996* SI 1996/972 The Stationery Office 1996 ISBN 0 11 063884 0

51   *A guide to the Genetically Modified Organisms (Contained Use) Regulations 2000* L29 (Third edition) HSE Books 2000 ISBN 0 7176 1758 0

52   *The Specified Animal Pathogens Order 1998* SI 1998/463 The Stationery Office 1998 ISBN 0 11 065801 9

53   *The Importation of Animal Pathogens Order 1980* SI 1980/1212 The Stationery Office 1980 ISBN 0 11 007212 X

54   *The Data Protection Act 1998 Ch 29* The Stationery Office 1998 ISBN 0 10 542998 8

55   *A guide to the Reporting of Injuries, Diseases and Dangerous Occurrences Regulations 1995* L73 (Second edition) HSE Books 1999 ISBN 0 7176 2431 5

Further reading

Hazardous substances publications

The Chemicals (Hazard Information and Packaging for Supply) Regulations 2002 SI 2002/1689 The Stationery Office 2002 ISBN 0 11 042419 0

COSHH: A brief guide to the regulations. What you need to know about the Control of Substances Hazardous to Health Regulations 2002 (COSHH) Leaflet INDG136(rev3) HSE Books 2005 (single copy free or priced packs of 10 ISBN 0 7176 2982 1)

The idiot's guide to CHIP 3: Chemicals (Hazard Information and Packaging for Supply) Regulations 2002 Leaflet INDG350 HSE Books 2002 (single copy free or priced packs of 5 ISBN 0 7176 2333 5)

Selecting protective gloves for work with chemicals: Guidance for employers and health and safety specialists Leaflet INDG330 HSE Books 2000 (single copy free or priced packs of 15 ISBN 0 7176 1827 7)

Related publications

Biological monitoring in the workplace: Information for employees on its application to chemical exposure Leaflet INDG245 HSE Books 1997 (single copy free or priced packs of 15 ISBN 0 7176 1450 6)

Five steps to risk assessment Leaflet INDG163(rev1) HSE Books 1998 (single copy free or priced packs of 10 ISBN 0 7176 1565 0)

General methods for sampling and gravimetric analysis of respirable and inhalable dust MDHS14/3 (Third edition) HSE Books 2000 ISBN 0 7176 1749 1 (see also other publications in the HSE MDHS series)

Electronic versions of current methods in the MDHS series can be downloaded from www.hse.gov.uk/pubns/mdhs/index.htm

Further information on the MDHS series, including the full revision history of each method, can be found at www.hsl.gov.uk/publications/methods-determination.htm

Publications on particular risks

There is a space here for only a small selection, please consult HSE for details of any other guidance produced for your industry.

Code of Practice for the safe use of pesticides on farms and holdings (available free from Information Services Branch, Pesticides Safety Directorate, Mallard House, King's Pool, 3 Peasholme Green, York YO1 7PX Tel: 01904 455733 or it can be downloaded from www.pesticides.gov.uk)

Health and safety in motor vehicle repair HSG67 HSE Books 1991
ISBN 0 7176 0483 7

Infection at work: Controlling the risk HSE 2003 Web only version available at at
www.hse.gov.uk/pubns/infection.pdf

*Legionnaires' disease. The control of legionella bacteria in water systems.
Approved Code of Practice and guidance* L8 (Third edition) HSE Books 2000
ISBN 0 7176 1772 6

Preventing asthma at work. How to control respiratory sensitisers L55 HSE Books
1994 ISBN 0 7176 0661 9

*The safe use of pesticides for non-agricultural purposes. Control of Substances
Hazardous to Health Regulations 1994. Approved Code of Practice* L9 (Second
edition) HSE Books 1995 ISBN 0 7176 0542 6

Working alone in safety: Controlling the risks of solitary work Leaflet
INDG73(rev) HSE Books 1998 (single copy free or priced packs of 15 ISBN 0
7176 1507 3)

Working safely with solvents: A guide to safe working practices Leaflet INDG273
HSE Books 1998 (single copy free)

Publications relevant to the principles in Schedule 2A

*Assessing and managing risks at work from skin exposure to chemical agents:
Guidance for employers and health and safety specialists* HSG205 HSE Books
2001 ISBN 0 7176 1826 9

*Choice of skin care products for the workplace: Guidance for employers and
health and safety specialists* HSG207 HSE Books 2001 ISBN 0 7176 1825 0

Controlling airborne contaminants in the workplace British Occupational Hygiene
Society Technical Guide 7 BOHS 1987 ISBN 0 90 592742 7

*Cost and effectiveness of chemical protective gloves for the workplace: Guidance
for employers and health and safety specialists* HSG206 HSE Books 2001
ISBN 0 7176 1828 5

BS EN ISO 6385: 2004 *Ergonomic principles in the design of work systems* British
Standards Institution

Industrial ventilation: A manual of recommended practice (25th edition) American
Conference of Governmental Industrial Hygienists (ACGIH) 2004
ISBN 1 882417 52 6

An introduction to local exhaust ventilation HSG37 (Second edition) HSE Books
1993 ISBN 0 7176 1001 2

Respiratory protective equipment at work: A practical guide HSG53 (Third
edition) HSE Books 2005 ISBN 0 7176 2904 X

PD 5304:2000 *Safe use of machinery* British Standards Institution

BS EN ISO 14738: 2002 *Safety of machinery. Anthropometric requirements for
the design of workstations at machinery* British Standards Institution

Further information

HSE priced and free publications are available by mail order from HSE Books, PO Box 1999, Sudbury, Suffolk CO10 2WA Tel: 01787 881165 Fax: 01787 313995 Website: www.hsebooks.co.uk (HSE priced publications are also available from bookshops and free leaflets can be downloaded from HSE's website: www.hse.gov.uk.)

For information about health and safety ring HSE's Infoline Tel: 0845 345 0055 Fax: 0845 408 9566 e-mail: hseinformationservices@natbrit.com or write to HSE Information Services, Caerphilly Business Park, Caerphilly CF83 3GG.

British Standards are available from BSI Customer Services, 389 Chiswick High Road, London W4 4AL Tel: 020 8996 9001 Fax: 020 8996 7001 e-mail: cservices@bsi-global.com Website: www.bsi-global.com

The Stationery Office publications are available from The Stationery Office, PO Box 29, Norwich NR3 1GN Tel: 0870 600 5522 Fax: 0870 600 5533 e-mail: customer.services@tso.co.uk Website: www.tso.co.uk (They are also available from bookshops.)

The Environment Agency (England and Wales) has a general enquiry line on 08708 506 506 or visit www.environment-agency.gov.uk

For Scotland, the Public Affairs Department of the Scottish Environment Protection Agency, on 01786 457700, handles general enquiries, or visit www.sepa.org.uk

Under the Reporting of Injuries, Diseases and Dangerous Occurrences Regulations 1995, all accidents, diseases and dangerous occurrences can now be reported to a central point. Send RIDDOR reports to the Incident Contact Centre, Caerphilly Business Park, Caerphilly CF83 3GG Tel: 0845 300 9923 Fax: 0845 300 9924 Website: www.riddor.gov.uk e-mail: riddor@natbrit.com

M224293

Printed and published by the Health and Safety Executive   04/05   C150